Joanne,
May tho 'FARCE
Terry Braverman
9/15/02

WHEN THE GOING GETS TOUGH, THE TOUGH LIGHTEN UP!
How To Be Happy In Spite Of It All

by
Terry Braverman

Mental Floss™ Publications
3865 S. Grand View Blvd.
Box 661037
Los Angeles, CA 90066

©1998 Second printing (revised)
©1998 Third printing

Publisher's Cataloging in Publication Data
Braverman, Terry 1953–
When the going gets tough, the tough lighten up/ Terry Braverman.
p. cm.
Includes bibliographical references and illustrations.
1. Psychology (humor) 2. Success 3. Interpersonal relations I. Title
MF304B27
158.33
Library of Congress Catalog Card Number: 97-93424
ISBN Number: 0-9657395-1-1

this book is dedicated
to my mother
for giving me
love, strength, and a
relatively easy birth process

CONTENTS

ACKNOWLEDGEMENTS

First and foremost, I want to thank God for making it all possible!

I want to thank my dearest friends for tolerating my incessant preoccupation with this book from start to finish: Michael Horn, Marilyn Joyce, Molly Diament, Rafael Beer, Louise Lanning, and Tom and Rina Daly. Thank you for your love and support!

I want to thank Susan Jeffers, Dr. Bernie Siegal, Terry Paulson, Dr. A. Jayne Major, Dyane Mohr, and Susan Levin for their constructive feedback while the book was a work in progress.

I want to thank all the people who contributed to the content of this book, from people who fed me great ideas, quotes and anecdotes, to publishers who granted me permission to use the aforementioned material.

Finally, I want to thank my "supporting cast" who helped create the "look" of the book:

Printer: Bookcrafters
Editor: Vicki St. George
Book design: Laura Shapiro
Book cover designer: Lightbourne Images
Illustrators: Noel Pugh, Gabe Martin, and Nick Hobart

BRAVERMAN'S "MIRTHQUAKE" PREPAREDNESS TEST

How much do you apply humor in your life? In recognition of the value of humor for our overall well-being, this simply serves as an indicator for you. After each statement, circle the number that most accurately depicts your level of mirthability. Be honest with yourself—nobody is watching!

> 5—almost always
> 4—frequently
> 3—sometimes
> 2—seldom
> 1—almost never

1. My family, friends and co-workers would say my sense of humor is one of my greatest assets.
   5 4 3 2 1

2. I find time to take a "humor break" every day (e.g. read cartoons, watch comedy, play with kids/pets).
   5 4 3 2 1

3. I laugh at myself easily.
   5 4 3 2 1

4. I am comfortable laughing out loud with others.
   5 4 3 2 1

5. I share humorous stories and insights with others.
   5 4 3 2 1

6. I apply humor in my work environment.
   5 4 3 2 1

7. I can enjoy an occasional ribbing from others.
   5   4   3   2   1

8. I consciously look for humor during the course of each day.
   5   4   3   2   1

9. People have difficulty staying angry at me because of my humor.
   5   4   3   2   1

10. I spontaneously laugh even when I am by myself.
    5   4   3   2   1

11. I use humor to help others gain perspective on their problems.
    5   4   3   2   1

12. I can find humor even in times of adversity.
    5   4   3   2   1

TOTAL SCORE:

60 POINTS	You're kidding, or you flunked arithmetic
50 to 60	Life of the party
40 to 50	Good dinner companion
30 to 40	Minor attitude adjustment needed; do lunch with a clown
20 to 30	Major attitude adjustment needed; wear a clown nose to your next board meeting
0 to 20	Severe case of CS (Chronic Seriousness); rent a gorilla suit and crash a wedding

CHAPTER 1

YES, WE'RE HAVING FUN...BUT WHY?
How To Lighten Up And Revitalize Your Spirit

"A merry heart doeth good like medicine, but a broken spirit drieth the bone."—Proverb 17:22

"WIPE THAT STUPID GRIN OFF YOUR FACE!" How many of us ever heard that during our formative years? The message from our families comes through like a somber TV commercial: "And now, a word from our sponsors. Having fun is a serious offense, punishable by solitary confinement. Don't think and jive!"

As a child I always felt that adulthood was an unappealing destination, and resisted attempts by my elders to convert me to solemnity. I felt like I had to put my inner child up for adoption to become an adult. To some extent, we all bought into it; I trust this book will serve as a debriefing and help us realize the value of lightening up to improve ourselves on all levels.

Amidst the break speed hustle of our hectic lifestyles, we have forgotten how to play. Why do I feel that play is so important? When the going gets tough, it gives us a larger context for living. It reminds us of the simpler joys of being spontaneous and allowing our thoughts and actions to happily flow, which can spark creative ideas and even resolve serious problems. It lifts us out of the box of limitation and routine into open space and freedom. It puts a new frame on reality and can change the way we view the whole picture. It positively alters our entire physiology; we breathe deeper and take in more aliveness. It gives us perspective, and returns us to the adventure of living with wider eyesight and greater insight.

JACK-OF-ALL-SURGEONS. It's Christmas of '87, and I'm not in a ho-ho-holiday spirit. Hawaiian travel plans were jettisoned because my girlfriend needed surgery. She was especially dispirited over having to relinquish a Hawaiian beach for a hospital bed, so during her entire stay I brought holly and folly to her hospital room.

On Christmas day, I came into the room wearing surgical attire with Ray-Ban sunglasses, doing an impression of Jack Nicholson as a surgeon: "Hey man, we're gonna do some serious healing around here..." I pulled out a nail clipper and in that nasally Nicholson voice said, "Let's start with an incision of the spinal cortex."

My girlfriend was laughing so hard I thought her stitches would burst across the room. It may have caused her some physical discomfort, but it was mirthful medicine. Her doctor was impressed with how quickly she healed, and insisted that I show him how to impersonate Jack Nicholson to treat future patients.

LEADERS DIGEST. The positive impact that laughter has on our well-being is nothing new. Throughout history, clowns, fools and court jesters plied their trade not only to entertain, but to heal people, impart wisdom, and exercise diplomacy, acting as ambassadors to other kingdoms to build goodwill and defuse conflict. The court jesters pranced around the monarchies with patented blends of whim and wit. It was their privilege to say whatever they wished. Usually a great ruler was surrounded by flatterers, and only from the jester did he ever hear the truth.

The jester's business was to tickle the royal funnybone, divert the king from the tedium of his daily affairs, and provide a slightly skewed yet enlightening perspective on those affairs of the court. Jesters also assisted his Majesty's digestion, rubbing the royal tummy the right way with their lively presence at the dining table. "Laughter is one of the most important aids to digestion with which we are acquainted," said the Prussian professor Hufeland. "The custom in vogue among our ancestors, of inciting laughter by jesters and buffoons, was founded on true medical principles. Cheerful and joyous companions are invaluable at meals; obtain such, if possible, for the nourishment received amid mirth is productive of light and healthy blood." Studies have shown that environment is a key determinant to healthy digestion (you will discover in the Family Follies chapter).

SHIFT HAPPENS WITH HUMOR. Native American tribes have sacred clowns or divine tricksters, sometimes called medicine teachers, who perform zany antics and use reverse psychology to rejuvenate the sick and dispirited ones, teaching wisdom through humor. They are known for teaching lessons that lift their brethren out of chronic seriousness. This can break up old patterns of behavior and restore balance in people.

The trickster's pranks are not cruel or self-serving; in fact, the people feel honored to be chosen for a trick that conveys valuable spiritual lessons. In their typically eccentric manner, the trickster seeks not to supply the answers, but to inspire revelations in others.

One very despondent man recounts an experience with his medicine teacher: "I learned my first lesson in Mexico, when Joaquin, my medicine teacher, wanted me to see how ridiculous my seriousness had become. We spent one whole day gathering dried cow dung and other animal waste, carefully placing them in an old tin bucket. The next day we spent mixing it all together.

"After this was completed, I was told to mark a circle in the earth with string and a stick, making sure that the circle was perfectly round. Then Joaquin told me to fill the groove in the soil with the fecal mixture. I was very careful to make a perfect circle and not to let any of the circle be crooked. Joaquin praised my work and how careful I had been during the two day process. He then told me to enter the circle and sit in the center until I understood the value of the lesson.

"I sat there for several hours, thinking that perhaps this was a way to contact the Spirit World. Joaquin took one look at me, and rolled on the ground in side-splitting laughter. He laughed so hard he could not speak! I was fascinated, while still sitting in my circle of poop, serious as ever.

"In between his guffaws, the trickster uttered the words that taught me my lesson. 'For the past three days you've been examining other people's shit!' he screamed. 'Now you've surrounded yourself with it and you can't even see how ridiculous you look.' I started to laugh at myself, and wondered how Joaquin managed to keep a straight face for two days.

"It finally came to me that I had spent the previous days worrying about the problems of others. All of these worries, in effect, had left me sitting in a circle of other people's mental garbage. The lesson hit me hard, and I laughed until I was aching and tears ran down my face. It has taken me many years to master the lesson, and I still get sucked into the drama of others at times. But when I do, Joaquin will come to me and dissolve my seriousness with more trickster antics."

SLAPSTICK AS AN APPETIZER. Are trickster tactics unnecessarily silly and extreme? Hunkering down with a pile of manure may not be your idea of enlightenment, but we all know how difficult it can be to overcome bouts of lingering seriousness. I recall a time when I went through a relationship breakup and couldn't shake the blues. It manifested in the form of a chest cold that lasted for two weeks. A couple of comical friends invited me out for dinner one night so I reluctantly tagged along.

The restaurant was jammed and there was a thirty minute wait to get a table, so I sought out the restroom while my friends put us on the waiting list. I returned and sat with my two friends for what seemed like an eternity. I started to go into a bit of a snit over the long wait when this announcement came over the speaker system: "Stooges, party of three. Stooges." My two friends jumped up and yelled, "That's us!" and proceeded to do a spontaneous Stooges bit. People around us were hysterical with laughter. I quickly leaped to my feet and added to the bit by gently tugging on the ears of my friends and steering them into the dining room. My chest cold went away, and the joy of mirth making returned to me for the first time in a long time!

UNRESTRAINING ORDER. Today we are all afflicted to some degree with SDS (spontaneity deficiency syndrome). It is appalling in our society how much we miss merry-making opportunities by censoring our own spontaneity.

"Well, I'm trying to find time to be spontaneous," a harried business acquaintance once muttered. Indigenous people tend to release their emotions and heal what ails them in the moment, through singing, dancing, chanting, and wearing wild costumes. How many of us would feel comfortable doing that in front of our families? We have largely suppressed or forgotten spontaneity in the maze of our busyness, our plans, our rational thinking, our control mechanisms. SDS is a major cause of stress in our world.

When we are in a lot of physical pain it takes some strong medicine to get relief. If the pain is emotional, we often need a strong jolt to regain our perspective. A dose of silly nonsense may just do the trick to heal the hurts of the heart.

I cringe when I see people being scolded for acting too silly. It can be inappropriate in certain situations, but more often than not it's the "grow up and get serious" parental mentality at work, stifling the natural stress relief of playful expression. The word *silly* comes from the Old English word *saelig*, which was a blessing—it meant "to be happy, prosperous and wise." On the other hand, let's look at where the word *adult* came from—*adulterate*, meaning "to corrupt, debase, or make impure."

MEDITATE IN THE RUSH HOUR. Several years ago a friend of mine went to see a meditation guru from India speak at a local auditorium. At the close of the event, the master was taking questions from the audience. One person asked, "What is the best form of meditation when you're feeling upset?" The guru sat and ruminated for about a minute with a smile spreading across his face, then said, "There is no best way to meditate. If one is stuck in rush hour traffic on the Hollywood Freeway and fully embraces the experience in a pure state of awareness and acceptance, that is meditation."

And so it is with humor. We need not change, alter or avoid an experience to find the humor in it. Instead of resisting it, humor can embrace the experience as it is, the way it is, from another perspective and allows us to move through it more fluidly.

LOOSE ID. Think of people you know who convey a strong sense of self-esteem. Do they also have a well-developed sense of humor? I would bet the house that they do. They may not dye their hair a primary color and go cartwheeling down an aisle in a public library wearing a clown suit, but they have a certain perspective that keeps them loose and limber.

People who suffer from chronic seriousness can become brittle when faced with obstacles, which then undermines their self-esteem. With a strong humorous perspective we're not as fazed by such obstacles. We can tackle our challenges diligently and lucidly, yet take ourselves lightly.

SAVED BY THE BELL. A therapist I know told me she was very glum after her husband died. She was burned out, having thrown herself totally into the relationship and had nothing left to give to herself. "I didn't know what to do with myself," she recalled. "I had spoken to my therapist and asked her if that is what I had been doing all my life, and she said yes. I was really in the pits. I felt like giving up, and seriously considered suicide. Then the phone rang. I picked up the receiver, and I suddenly burst out laughing, because I had this vision of myself lying in a coffin, the phone rings, and I say, 'Just a minute, I can't die yet. I have to answer the phone.'

"I shared this vision with the friend who was calling me, and she was in stitches. I realized how ludicrous the whole thing was. At that moment a life long pattern of nothing but giving, giving, giving changed because I gave myself the gift of laughter."

COHERE THE SEVERE. Generating a state of joy helps others move through a sense of loss and tragedy. I was once hired to speak at a company's annual retreat, and just prior to my introduction it was announced that a very beloved employee of the company had suddenly died. When a woman came on stage to introduce me, she was in tears, and there were audible wails and moans emanating from the audience. She mumbled and stumbled through my introduction, and still weeping, said, "So here to talk about...(blows her nose) humor in the... (sniffles) workplace..... Terry Braverman." I walked on stage pondering a line from a Shakespearean tragedy: "Oh death, where is thy sting?"

At a total loss for words in that moment, I took a long pause and a deep breath. Finally the words filtered through me: "I know this is a difficult time for all of you, and I want to acknowledge the sadness and the grief you are feeling right now. This must have been a very special person who touched all of you in some way. I was wondering if any of you would like to come up here to the microphone and share some of those special moments you had with Corrine—shared moments of warmth, joy, humor, or maybe something she said that lightened up your day."

After about 15-20 seconds, a hand went up, and I asked her to step up to the microphone. She spoke of a time when Corrine was promoted to supervisor of the department, and how Corrine was concerned about becoming the boss to people who had been her co-workers.

So Corrine decided to call a meeting with her former co-workers the next day. When the room had filled up at the meeting, Corrine strutted into the room, wearing a pin-striped suit with a Yankee Doodle hat and said, "This great department is a democracy, and I run it now."

My audience broke up laughing at this story! Then several hands went up in the audience, and I had four or five more people share heartwarming experiences they had with Corrine. The tears of sorrow for their deceased colleague transformed into tears of joy, and I was able to proceed with my presentation.

A LAUGH OR DEATH SITUATION. Humor can thrive in the harshest environments. The book *Laughter In Hell*, by Steve Lipman, documents the use of humor during the Holocaust. There was nothing funny about the Holocaust and the intense suffering experienced by so many people. But survivors of the Nazi death camps cultivated humor out of psychological necessity.

A Dutch Jew by the name of Rachella Velt Meekcoms recounted times when she would stage vaudeville shows in Auschwitz with other inmates: "In spite of all our agony and pain we never lost our ability to laugh at ourselves and our miserable situation. We had to make jokes to survive and save ourselves from deep depression. We mimicked top overseers, I did impersonations about camp life and somebody did a little tap dance, different funny, crazy things. The overseers slipped into the barracks while we weren't looking, and instead of giving us punishment they were laughing their heads off." Rachella survived the Holocaust.

Across occupied Europe during World War II, humor thrived in the work of the resistance forces. Arrows at highway crossings were turned around and street signs switched, creating utter confusion among Hitler's army. Cooks stirred laxatives into the food for German troops, and "Only for Germans" signs were removed from places of entertainment and hung from lamp posts.

PASTOR ODs ON LAUGHTER. Illness and injury are not considered to be a laughing matter, but when it comes to religion, spirituality, healing, and the afterlife, a growing number of ministers are extolling the virtues of humor and laughter.

One pastor experienced firsthand the healing effects of laughter. His car was crunched by another vehicle while driving on the freeway, and he was rushed to a hospital in serious pain. Painkilling shots were administered almost every hour. One time the pastor rang for the nurse to get another pain shot. It took all the strength he had to roll over and ready himself for her arrival. When he heard footsteps enter the room, he said, "I think this area here isn't too bad," pointing to an exposed part of his backside. There was an awkward silence that followed his remark. His face paled as he rolled over slowly to see who had actually come into the room—it was one of his 22-year-old female parishioners!

He apologized and tried to strike up a conversation with her, but she was terribly embarrassed and left quickly. The incongruity of the situation started to seep in and soon the pastor was laughing uncontrollably, tears streaming down his face. He was laughing so hard that when the nurse came in, he couldn't tell her what had just happened. She promised to return in a few minutes, after he had calmed down.

The pastor had regained his composure when the nurse came back. But when she asked what had occurred, the pastor erupted again into laughter. The nurse giggled from watching him laugh so much, and again said she would check back in 15 minutes. This scenario repeated itself three more times, and by the time he told her the story, the pain was gone. The endorphins kicked in, and he didn't need any medication for several hours. He claimed that it was the turning point in his recovery.

PLAYING AND PRAYING. "Humor," wrote theologian Reinhold Niebuhr, "is, in fact, a prelude to faith; and laughter is the beginning of prayer. Laughter must be heard in the outer courts of religion, and the echoes of it should resound in the sanctuary. Humor is concerned with the immediate incongruities of life and faith the ultimate ones."

I could never understand why most churches and synagogues are like morgues, or sanctuaries of terminal seriousness. If people come together in communion to worship God, Spirit, the Source, the Life Force, whatever you name it, isn't that cause for celebration? Granted, there are times we come to seek solace in the silence of a quiet sanctuary, and it's good to provide those moments. But to honor whatever it is that imbues us with energy, I say sing, dance and laugh; rejoice in our aliveness and oneness with it all.

"Lots of people believe they have to be serious or sorrowful to be responsive to God," said Rev. Margaret Stortz, First Church of Religious Science, Oakland, CA. "But God is more clearly expressed through our joy than our suffering. There is no reason why humor can't be included in one's spiritual practice."

Rev. Michael Boblett of the Marin Fellowship of Unitarians, San Rafael, CA, agrees that humor is healing. Boblett has even acted as court jester at the local Renaissance fair. He occasionally lectures on the value of humor and laughter in church, and views them as sacred.

Some of us may have feelings of guilt over having fun, and believe that we should be serious and "responsible." Remember this: Guilt is a wonderful thing to waste! Trust me—I know this one well, because I was raised Jewish, and if you were raised Jewish you may have a belief that guilt is hereditary. If you were raised Catholic, it's educational.

JEST THE TRUTH FROM JESUS. The eminent *Peanuts* cartoonist, Charles Schulz, once remarked, "Nobody would have been invited to dinner as much as Jesus was unless he was interesting and had a sense of humor."

He must have had a whale of an appetite as well. Both Jesus and his disciples were notable for their eating and drinking (Luke 5:33), and provided the basis for a humorous rejoinder, to the effect that his critics could not be pleased: "For John the Baptist has come eating no bread and drinking no wine, and you say, 'He has a demon.' The Son of Man has come eating and drinking, and you say, 'Behold, a glutton and a drunkard, a friend of tax collectors and sinners!' Yet wisdom is justified by all her children." (Luke 7:31-35)

Is it possible that there was a mirthful side to the Prince of Peace? In studying the Synoptic gospels, I detect an irony and wit from his teachings that, if taken literally, would render them meaningless and therefore debunks the myth that Jesus was somber and always to be taken seriously.

I concluded that Jesus understood the value of humor in opening the minds and hearts of the people to reveal truth. For example, when he said "not to cast pearls before swine," it was a humorous way of saying, "Why bother attempting to enlighten the rigidly unreceptive?" It appears he was adding an additional twist of irony as well, considering it was for a Jewish audience to whom rejection of pork was deep-seated in those days.

Jesus once said, "To enter the kingdom of heaven, see the world through the eyes of a child." He understood that most kids have an innocent, open and unfettered perspective of the world. They laugh frequently (60-400 times daily, according to studies), which may in part explain their high energy level. We can learn much from their quirky sense of wonderment and humor. Spending time with a child can help us broaden our own perspective and not take the world so seriously (more on childlike humor in the "Family Follies" chapter).

IS THERE A LAUGH AFTER DEATH? Humor or no humor, eventually we all seem to shuffle off the mortal coil. Speculation is fertile ground for absurdity, and I often speculate on what the afterlife would be like. Is there a bridge one crosses to get to the other side? If so, is there a toll booth at the entrance, and will I need exact change? Should I wear Ray-Bans if I go through a tunnel of light? Some who have had near death experiences claim to have gone through such a tunnel, only to return to the material world. Couldn't they make a living on the other side? Why else would they come back? Since I've been single so far in this life, will I merge with another soul in the afterlife, or will I join an out of body singles club? Imagine not being concerned about what the other looks like, or whether they snore in their sleep, eat crackers in bed, or leave the toilet seat up. But where do you take someone on a first date?

Will I run into any creditors in the afterlife and have to make additional karmic payments? Are there any good pension plans in the afterlife? Should I bring a snack in case I get hungry on the other side, should I take a sweater with me, will my mother still expect me to write...?

The Borderline, by Gabe Martin, borderln@cts.com

CHAPTER 2

WARNING: LAUGHTER MAY BE HAZARDOUS TO YOUR AILMENTS
How To Boost Your Amuse System

"The art of medicine consists of amusing the patient while nature cures the disease."—Voltaire

Would it be beyond medical standards for a doctor to "needle" patients in their "jocular" vein for better health and overall well being? Some doctors insist that up to 60% of all medical treatments are preventable. Some people insist that up to 70% of all doctors are preventable. I say that not to criticize doctors or suggest their obsolescence, but to elicit a chuckle and encourage each of us to shoulder greater responsibility for our health and well being.

Akin to the decline of full service gas stations, there has been a gradual dip in the number of visits to primary health care physicians, and a shift towards self-servicing our health as the new millennium approaches. Many of us perceive preventive medicine in terms of a healthy diet, sufficient rest and regular exercise, but a mental tune-up needs to be incorporated in order to keep our inner engine humming—and that includes humor. Humor provides an attitude lubricant that not only assists our capacity to stay physiologically fit, but also helps to keep us energized, creative, loose and flexible.

It would be nice if a vitamin company came out with a guffaw tablet to ingest whenever we're faced with setbacks, or to relieve any kind of mental constipation. Magically, we'd laugh at everything from bankruptcies to broken fingernails. Yet there are strategies we can apply to mitigate trying circumstances and maintain some perspective. To perceive those situations in a humorous light requires willingness, skill and discipline (or "blissipline," as I prefer to call it).

HE MUST HAVE DIED LAUGHING. In our time, the person most responsible for introducing humor's healing power to the mainstream is Norman Cousins. The former editor of the *Saturday Review* and a UCLA professor, Cousins was diagnosed with a collagen disease that had never been cured before. The doctors gave him only six months to live. Rather than succumb to a state of gloom and resignation, he resolved to live gleefully in what appeared to be the abbreviated remainder of his life span.

At his request, people brought to his bedside funny books, tapes, cartoons, gag gifts, and anything that might provoke laughter. After just a few weeks of devouring a steady diet of comedy (with no other dietary or medicinal changes), his disease went into remission! And his sense of humor became a bit wacky.

One morning Norman Cousins was eating his breakfast when the nurse stepped into the room and handed him an empty specimen bottle, saying she'd swing back around to collect it in a few minutes. After she left, he took the apple juice that came with his breakfast and emptied it into the specimen bottle. When the nurse returned she examined the sample and said, "It looks a little cloudy today, Mr. Cousins." Norman picked up the bottle and shrieked, "By George, you're right. Let's run it through again!" and proceeded to swig from the bottle. He had to stop, though, because he was concerned that the unsuspecting nurse might keel over from the spectacle.

The raucous laughter of Norman Cousins continually reverberated throughout the ward, which delighted the nurses but disturbed the patients. Hospital administration politely gave him the boot, so he checked into a hotel, which was far more environmentally friendly for outbursts of mirth. His life, which lasted for another 15 years, inspired many in search of pain relief and healing. I saw Norman Cousins receive a humanitarian award about three weeks before he passed on—a man who appeared to be vigorous and in good health. He must have died laughing.

SIDE-SPLITTING EFFECTS. There are scientifically proven benefits to those hearty yuk-yuks:

Benefit #1: Laughter is non-fattening, with no ill side effects. It's pretty hard to eat and laugh at the same time; if you do, you will probably lose all your friends. Instead of harmful side effects, you may get side-splitting effects, but nothing that will land you in intensive care.

Benefit #2: Laughter increases blood circulation, allowing faster delivery of oxygen and nutrients to the cells than Federal Express. And, its F.O.B. (free on board)

Benefit#3: Laughter aids digestion and elimination. I won't touch this one.

Benefit #4: Laughter amplifies respiration. A good belly laugh can elevate oxygen intake by as much as fivefold, and will keep your respiratory system well ventilated.

Benefit #5: Laughter activates muscles. Like an internal workout, giggles will work the muscles around your mouth first, then your chest and abdominal muscles, diaphragm, etc. Dr. William F. Fry, a Stanford professor emeritus who pioneered research into the physiology of mirth and laughter, said that 100 laughs is aerobically equivalent to an average of 10 minutes on a rowing machine in the gym!

Benefit #6: Laughter releases endorphins, a natural pain killer (and less expensive than codeine).

Benefit #7: Laughter connects both hemispheres of the brain. According to Dr. Kenneth Pelletier, author of *Mind As Healer, Mind As Slayer*, "The only two activities that create total brain symmetry are laughter and orgasms." Doing both simultaneously is a real kick!

Benefit #8: Laughter can boost various components of the immune system. Dr. Lee Berk at Loma Linda University has conducted recent studies that lend credibility to this statement. In one of his studies done in 1993, a group of healthy people had their immune responses monitored while viewing a pres-elected 60 minute humor video. Multiple blood samples were taken before, during, after the video, and into the next day. The group showed significant increases in immune cells, natural killer cell activity and antibodies. While studies such as this are preliminary, they demonstrate the connection between "feel good" emotions, such as laughter, and the immune system. Dr. Berk's research indicates that laughter may also decrease so-called stress hormones like epinephrine and cortisol, which can suppress the immune system.

Benefit #9: The cathartic effects of laughter vanquish emotional tension, as demonstrated by the state of relaxation that follows mirthful laughter. When the going gets tough, feelings such as anxiety, anger and depression can usurp our sense of well being. They demand a serious attitude; humor banishes the fear, uptightness and severity necessary to maintain a serious position. A major factor in the onset of heart attacks is a sudden, intense rush of anger. Humor and rage are antithetical. In any situation, the birth of mirth diminishes the futility of hostility.

HUMOR SAYS NO TO DRUGS. In the humor seminars and workshops that I give, it thrills me to witness accumulated stress draining from the faces and bodies of participants. I have received a number of positive letters from various companies and organizations, but none were more gratifying than the following:

Dear Terry,

Your seminar on humor was great. I particularly related to your discussion on stress, and others sharing their experiences of how stress had manifested itself. I identified totally. Since your seminar, I've had no more headaches, no more clenched jaws, no more valium, Xanax, Halcion or sleepless nights. I've shared my experience with co-workers. Thanks for a real eye-opening exchange.

Larry Simons

I recently spoke with Mr. Simons, three years after the fact. He is still free of the aforementioned ailments and takes no medication. I think of the workshop as a collective creation between myself and the participants, where credit is due to no one in particular other than the group intent. Making such a dramatic impact on Mr. Simons' health says a lot for the value of humor and play. Clearly, there was a shift in his thinking that took place in an atmosphere of mirth, causing a positive physiological response. Dr. Deepak Chopra once said, "Our thoughts, without reservation, tend to make us healthy or sick." I might add that our reservations (doubts), without changing our thoughts, tend to make us sick.

Studies suggest that depression can play a major role in the onset of cancer, the second major killer disease. The enjoyment of mirthful laughter can make us less susceptible to cancer. In times of tragedy, we instinctively turn to comedy for its uplifting effects. For the cancer patient who feels the suffering and mental anguish associated with their condition, humor can lift the spirit and reduce suffering for the moment, if not permanently.

JOKE SIGNALS. Someone came up with the equation that tragedy + time = humor. Sometimes tragedy and humor sleep in the same hospital bed, with inspiring results. This story came from a new friend in cyberspace: "At age 12 I developed a life-threatening case of pneumonia, and was taken to the hospital by ambulance. (The family was later amused when they saw my name in our weekly village newspaper because their 'rescue squad' of journalists paid me a visit.) The emergency medical technicians and I were talking and cracking jokes, so when we arrived at the hospital they told my parents I was OK, while the reverse was happening.

"The infection grabbed hold of me so quickly that within several hours after admitting me to ICU, my parents were called back to the hospital to say good-bye. Even a priest was praying beside my bed; being Jewish, that didn't upset me in the slightest, as I figured I'd need all the help I could get. Besides, it was a Catholic hospital.

"When mom and dad came in to bid me adieu, something magical took place. My father brought in and showed me a monstrous menu from a restaurant I'd always wanted to go to, then said that when I was feeling better we could have dinner there. He and I had a signal of sorts when we were having fun: One of us would raise our eyebrows up and down, then the other reciprocated in kind. Now the magic—after seeing the menu and hearing that I might try lion steak in the near future, I wiggled my eyebrows towards my father, and he did the same back at me. Somehow the crisis miraculously passed, and I recovered."

OPERATING WITH HUMOR. The breeding ground for humor is often found in adversity. This gives us a sense of the role that humor plays in our daily experience. Consider the television series *M.A.S.H.* Imagine if those characters were extremely sensitive and humorless. They would spend a great deal of time crying and agonizing over the blood, pain, and critical conditions of the soldiers who were carted in. They'd be doing a lot of hugging, consoling, and processing their feelings! Could they perform surgery and repair limbs in such a state of mind? Of course not. So they joked about their jobs and the frequently grotesque conditions they had to deal with. The so-called "gallows" humor they used would be off-putting in many instances, but for them it was the chosen mode of behavior that allowed them to get the job done.

When dealing with death and dying, agony and pain, humor furnishes the ultimate survival tools. Hospital scenarios can be both bizarre and amusing, as this nurse's story will attest: "We had a three-year-old boy brought into the emergency room by his mom, and he was complaining about an upset stomach. Upon evaluation and X-ray they discovered a toy stuck inside.

"The patient went to the operating room and during surgery the toy fell out—it was one of those battery powered toys and it was still running! I guess those energizer batteries really do keep going and going and going."

When we're feeling exhausted, depressed, or upset, our own batteries need to be recharged. My suggestion—take this chapter before you go to bed, and call me in the morning.

TIPS ON HEALING YOUR LOVED ONES
(AND THAT INCLUDES YOU)

- Bring them a pet or child to interact with, if possible.
- Give them comedy videos, tapes, books, cartoons, and funny greeting cards.
- Decorate their room with humorous and inspirational sayings, signs and funny photos.
- When you see them, wear outrageous clothing or props (clown nose, Groucho glasses...).
- Invite them to keep a joy or humor journal to remind them of the people, places, things and situations that make them smile or laugh.
- Hire me to perform celebrity impressions for them (a shameless plug).
- Keep in mind that humor may not always be appropriate—just give them your loving attention.

CHAPTER 3

WE INTERRUPT THIS PROGRAM TO BRING YOU A SPECIAL NEWS BULLETIN: LIFE IS GOOD!
How To Change Negative Patterns Of Behavior Immediately

"Do not burden yourselves with needless anxieties and concerns."
—Jesus (Easy for him to say!)

Some people think that I must have been funny since the day I was born. Not so—I did not boogie down the birth canal with a clown nose on, doing comedic impressions of other babies. My childhood was not particularly joyful. My father was diagnosed with lung cancer when I was just four years old. For the following eight years he was in and out of the hospital, and had six major operations, starting with his back. After each operation, the cancer returned, spreading to his pancreas, gall bladder and liver. The whites of his eyes were often a pale, sickly yellow. I grew up watching my father become progressively more gaunt and immobilized. Cancer finally claimed his life when I was 13.

The same year, I witnessed another traumatic incident. In the middle of a friend's bar mitzvah service, a man marched down the aisle of the temple, pulled out a gun and fatally shot the rabbi. People were screaming and I remember running out of the sanctuary absolutely terrified. It is ironic that after witnessing a death on a "stage," I chose to do my life's work on a stage (and I've died on stage myself a few times).

I often felt scared, vulnerable and unprotected as a child. The neighborhood bully would stalk me on the way to school, pelting me with snowballs in the winter and twigs in the summer. Then one day he moved away, and what a relief it was; better than any of my birthday parties! But a week later, a new bully succeeded the old bully. I think there was a summit meeting of the incoming and outgoing bullies, because the incoming bully knew he could pick on me right away and get away with it.

JUST MASSAGING MY BRAIN. I also had a fourth grade teacher by the name of Mrs. Flynn. She was an Olive Oyl look-alike with a pit bull demeanor. It seemed as though she always dressed in brown, wore brown shoes, toted a brown purse, transported herself in a brown car. Mrs. Flynn didn't pelt me with snowballs, but she had an amazing knack for catching me when I picked my nose in class. For additional humiliation, she mispronounced my name: "Teddy Beaverman, stop picking your nose!" The entire class snickered at me as I withered in my seat.

A negative program of helplessness and fear was being imprinted. Obviously I gave an impression of weakness, and there was a lot of fear around money in the family, with hospital bills piling up all the time. Thoughts and beliefs about lack and limitation ran rampant.

I look upon it now as a true blessing, because I'm living proof that negative programming can be transformed. Sharing my early hardships with others helps them to realize that no matter how painful their experiences have been, it is possible to break negative programming and live a more joyful life.

INTERRUPT US. Patterns of behavior can be interrupted and changed instantaneously. When people lock into recurring patterns of negative behavior, it may serve them better to have someone interrupt the pattern rather than sympathize with them, which reinforces the attention they inherit for acting out that pattern. Program interrupts (or pattern breakers, as I sometimes call them) can short circuit the pattern and inspire a more resourceful, positive state. An outrageous act, like sticking a clown nose on their face and having them look in a mirror, can alter their state of mind.

ALTERED STATE IN D.C. Jean Houston, a philosopher, human capacities researcher, and author of the book, *A Mythic Life*, was hired with other presenters to inspire creativity in Washington bureaucrats and help build a more people-centered society. On the way there, one of her co-presenters remarked, "This is no man's land (for the kind of healing work they do). Government bureaucrats spend their time rearranging the deck chairs on the Titanic. They're not going to listen to us." Jean Houston acknowledged the challenge ahead and said, "You're probably right. So, we'll have to alter their consciousness." "How?" her friend wondered aloud. "With jokes," she answered. "For me, laughter is the ultimate altered state. At the peak of roaring laughter, one exists, as in mid-sneeze, everywhere and nowhere, and is thus available to be blessed, evoked, and deepened. In the bag of tricks I've used over the years to bring people to other states of mind, I still find that for most, laughter remains the easiest way to begin moving beyond that half-awake state we call normal waking consciousness. So I'll open this august gathering with ten minutes of stand-up comedy. After much laughter and rib nudging, I'll look out over the audience—no more glacial stares, or supercilious smirks. 'Good,' I say to myself. They are ready for the next part."

HAVING A RIOT ON THE FREEWAY. Pattern breakers can give birth to a sense of levity in the face of adversity. In 1992, civil unrest broke out in Los Angeles. The radio blared the news—Mayor Bradley had just imposed a dusk to dawn curfew in the city. I was driving on the Hollywood freeway during the rush hour, traffic typically bumper to bumper. Looking out the passenger side window, I saw fires ablaze on the horizon. I detected smoke from burning buildings that saturated the already smoggy air. I glanced at my fellow commuters, alert to the fear engraved on their faces. Perhaps they were wondering if their houses and neighborhoods were ablaze as well.

The anxiety around me was starting to seep into my brain until I couldn't stand it anymore. Something must be done to ease the surrounding sense of despair! Do I leap out of the car and do a stand-up routine on the freeway? I'd probably get run over. Ah...my prop bag was behind the seat. I blindly groped around with my hand and pulled out a show stopper—a two-inch red clown nose! I stuck it on my face. People around me were doing double takes which said, "He must be a tourist. He doesn't know what's happening." I'm sure they were not wondering if I was available for children's parties. But when I smiled at them, they got the message. I wanted to let them know that in spite of the circumstances, we can take a moment to lighten up and suspend the downward spiral of distress.

The effect was remarkable. People laughed, smiled back, gave the thumbs up, honked horns, nudged their driving buddies and pointed at me. Kids jumped up and down in the back seats and giggled. People of all ages and backgrounds were sharing a moment of fun in the face of adversity. Truly it was one of the finest moments I've experienced!

DISARMING AND CHARMING. My fiery, provocative friend Andrea is a crusader for every environmental cause imaginable. You would probably find her leading a "save the slugs" rally. She also carries no inhibitions about expressing her distaste for authority figures. One time she was stopped for speeding. Bracing for the usually unpleasant experience of being ticketed, she found the officer to be disarmingly amiable and humorous, a clear pattern break for her. She even laughed when he told her some of the outrageous excuses people contrive for speeding.

They engaged in friendly conversation, and she curiously asked him if he liked his job. He said he liked it very much. She was mystified. How could someone enjoy dealing with peoples' resentment, frustration and fear? "What is it that you like about your work?" she inquired. "I save lives," he said poignantly. Andrea was floored by the officer's perspective, a perspective that made his work fulfilling and defused hostility among the people he encounters.

WHEN IN CRISIS, MAKE AN IMPRESSION. At my workshops, I talk about one of the ways to develop a humorous perspective, which is to ask yourself, if you're in a crisis or embarrassing situation, how would someone else react if they were in your shoes (a favorite comedian, famous person, etc.). And who would be better to ask that question to than the master impressionist himself—Rich Little.

A few years ago I interviewed Rich for a feature article in my newsletter, and he recalled a time when he used his talent to avoid a potentially dangerous encounter: "Once I was confronted by a bunch of thugs who I thought were going to beat me up. It was in south Florida and I was pretty scared, but within 15 minutes I had them laughing. I was doing my whole act and they were applauding! So I turned that around—I don't remember exactly how. I think I went into Louie Armstrong. But it was scary. They didn't know who I was, but when I started doing the impressions they lost their incentive to beat me up."

I asked him what other characters he assumes in those touchy situations. He replied, "Once in a while if I get angry I go into Kirk Douglas; if I do something silly I might go into Jack Benny, just out of embarrassment more than anything. One time I was in a supermarket and there was a pyramid stacked display with cans of peas. I just pulled one of the cans out of the bottom without thinking, and about 200 cans of peas fell down. There was a tremendous noise and the whole store ran over. I was standing there as Jack Benny, holding this can of peas, and I said to the crowd, 'Well, the ones on the bottom were on sale.' "

He continued: "I've done a lot of pranks on the phone using voices, like ordering room service as characters. I can figure out the popularity of (famous people) by how fast I could get it delivered. I once ordered a cheeseburger as Richard Nixon and it never came. But Cary Grant could get it there in about three minutes." Even if we don't have the comedic talent of a Rich Little, jumping into a character can help us put a better perspective on things.

EXCUSE ME THERAPY. In his book, *Unlimited Power*, Anthony Robbins gives an example of how to break a negative pattern: "I'm always amused at what happens when I conduct a therapy session at my home overlooking the ocean in California. When people arrive, the surroundings tend to put them in a positive state....I can see them drive up to the house, get out of the car, look around in obvious excitement, and proceed to the front door. They come upstairs, and we talk a little—it's all very pleasant and positive—and then I'll ask, 'Well, okay, what brings you here?' Immediately, I can see their shoulders slump, their facial muscles droop, their breathing become more shallow, their voice take on a tone of self-pity as they spin their tale of woe and decide to enter their 'troubled' state.

"The best way to deal with that pattern is to show them how easy it is to break. What I usually do is say very forcefully, almost in an angry or upset manner, 'Excuse me. We haven't started yet!' What happens? Immediately they say, 'Oh, I'm sorry,' sit straight up, resume normal breathing, posture, and facial expressions, and go back to feeling fine. The message comes through loud and clear."

We have the ability to break patterns simply by altering our physiology, and we can accomplish it in amusing ways. Try walking around the house, or around the block, looking upward for at least five minutes (or until you walk into a telephone pole; on second thought, better do this in a deserted parking lot or on a beach). Brush your teeth or feed yourself with the opposite hand—that's usually good for a chuckle. Coax yourself into making funny faces in the mirror when you're feeling low. It's harder to stay depressed when your body is telling you something else.

IT'S A LONG SHOT. Sometimes a pattern breaker will occur in our surroundings, and all we have to do is be open to it. Back in 1987, I was driving to a momentous television show audition, THE ONE I'D BEEN WAITING FOR, and my car broke down on a residential street in Burbank. I was very dejected and pounded my fists on the hood of the car, grunting and groaning.

All of a sudden, the sound of klippity-klop pricked my ears. I was startled by the sight of a man on a horse galloping by. It was so stupefying that not only did it immediately dismiss my upset, it piqued my curiosity. My intuition advised me to follow that horse. A block and a half later the horse made a left turn into an equestrian center. I informed the manager of my urgent situation, and they let me borrow a horse to ride to my audition...(Actually, what really happened is they let me use their phone so I could reschedule the audition, but doesn't the other scenario seem more dramatic?) Even though I ultimately didn't get the part, the opportunity remained intact.

TRIAL FOR DOLLARS. A pattern breaker can even be the start of a prolific career. In Charlie Chaplin's autobiography, he recalls his first, and unscheduled, step onto the stage: "I remember standing in the wings (offstage) when mother's voice cracked and went to a whisper. The audience began to laugh, sing falsetto, and to make catcalls. The noise increased until mother was obliged to walk off the stage. When she came into the wings, she was very upset and argued with the stage manager who, having seen me perform before mother's friends, said something about letting me go on in her place.

"In the turmoil I remember his leading me by the hand, and after a few explanatory words to the audience, leaving me on the stage alone, before the glare of footlights, faces and smoke. I started to sing, accompanied by the orchestra which fiddled about until it found my key. Halfway through, a shower of money poured onto the stage. Immediately, I stopped to announce that I would pick up the money first and sing afterward. This caused much laughter. Repeating the chorus, in all innocence, I imitated mother's voice cracking. I was surprised at the impact—there was laughter and cheers, then more money throwing. Then my mother came onto the stage to carry me off. Her presence evoked tremendous applause. That night was my first appearance on the stage, and my mother's last."

RADICAL SHEIK. One of the real gifts of humor is that it offers us an alternative response. Sheik Salim came from a wealthy Saudi Arabian family, but was surely an oddity among fellow dignitaries. On one particular occasion, he stunned a group of American corporate presidents hosting a banquet in his honor, by playing the harmonica instead of giving a speech.

Another time, he arrived in Cairo to find no rooms available at a five star hotel. Even a multi-millionaire's temper tantrums wouldn't have budged the situation; but that was not his style anyway. "If I play the French national anthem for you on my harmonica," he asked the surprised hotel manager, Madame de la Porte, "will you give me a room?" "That's a funny way to get a room," said the Madame. "It's the only way left," answered the pragmatic Salim. He played *Le Marseillaise* for her and she found him a room.

WORKING FOR PEANUTS. One day I was motoring down Venice Boulevard in Los Angeles, feeling upset about the lack of paid engagements I was booking at that time. While waiting for the green arrow in the turning lane, there was an elderly, leathery-skinned vendor strolling on the road divider, holding up a bag of peanuts. In the midst of being upset, the story of her facial features caught my eye.

Something possessed me to roll down my window and ask her how much she wanted for the peanuts. "Just one dollar," she replied. I gave her a dollar, and she proceeded to hand over the bag when a light went on in my head: "Don't give it to me. Give it to the person behind me," I said mischievously.

I watched the scenario unfold in my rear view mirror as the woman in the car behind me kept waving away the vendor, thinking she was trying to sell the peanuts to her. Finally the vendor just flung the bag of peanuts on the driver's lap, smiled and pointed to me. The driver then realized it was a practical joke, and smiled at the vendor. It was hilarious! After making the turn, I slowed up to catch her bemused reaction as she drove by. My upset had vanished, and who knows how it may have brightened her day.

THERE YOU GO AGAIN. Dr. Mark Goulston, author of the book *Get Out Of Your Own Way: Overcoming Self-Defeating Behavior*, spoke of the tendency for salespeople and consultants to gab too much about their product or service. If it appears that they are losing a prospective client's attention, they may speak faster as well, which turns the prospect off even more.

When this occurs, a pattern breaker may be in order. Dr. Goulston suggests saying this: "Gee, I'm doing it again!" Or you may want to try your Reagan impression:

"Well...there I go again...." This will short circuit the disinterested mentality on the part of the prospect, making he or she wonder what it is this salesperson is doing again. The person would then explain how they get carried away in their enthusiasm, talk too much and too fast, and fail to consult the prospect on what their needs and concerns might be. This confession can lead to a new opening in the business relationship.

HAIL TO THE THIEF. Some people use pattern breakers inadvertently. I read a story in the *Oakland Tribune* about a 101-year-old woman who was sitting alone in her living room one evening when an intruder broke the lock on her front door. He rushed over and began to tie her up in a chair.

The woman, seemingly unaware of what was taking place, responded as if he were an honored guest. She offered to make him coffee or tea, mentioned that she'd just cooked a fresh batch of cookies and encouraged him to try them. The thief-to-be was completely baffled by her kindness and lack of fear. It short circuited the accustomed pattern of a fearful response in his victims so much that he did an about-face and left without taking a thing!

SIT FOR LIFE. There is a great deal of controversy today regarding assisted suicide. The spiritual teacher Ram Dass was asked his view of euthanasia in a recent interview. He said, "I have no moral thing as to when people check out. I'm very reticent to take away people's freedom, and that's their freedom to kill themselves. But if somebody asks me, 'Should I kill myself?' I'd say, 'Well, it sounds like you're in an interesting time. Why don't you sit with that question for about 10 years and see.' " What a great yet gentle touch of irony to redirect negative thinking!

MELLOW DRAMA. Another technique I like to use is to express my upsets as a news report or sporting event. It steers the emotional charge down a pseudo-grandiose path, highlighting it to an absurdly dramatic level.

One time I was driving to Vegas with a friend and his car overheated. When we jumped out of the car, my bearded friend was obviously upset, so I pretended to hold a microphone and engaged him in a wild sportscaster parody of the situation: "And now, live from the Mojave desert, it's the Vegas 500, where front-runner Gregory Schulman has just pulled out of the competition. It's a devastating blow to Schulman, who was attempting to become the first ever Orthodox rabbi to win this race. Greg, in your own words, could you tell the viewing audience what went wrong?" Greg responded, "Well, I had a feeling that driving on Saturday just wouldn't work for me. It was a self-fulfilling prophesy."

EXECUTIVE DISORDER. One of our most revered American leaders personifies the marriage of humor and persistence to triumph over adversity. In his lifetime, he got fired from his job, failed in business, ran for the state legislature and lost, lost a re-election bid for Congress, twice ran for the Senate and lost, and was unsuccessful in an attempt to be nominated for vice president.

Despite the misfortunes, periods of extreme depression, and the death of three sons and a childhood sweetheart, he somehow was able to access a sense of humor to give him the courage to carry on. His name: Abraham Lincoln.

During the most dismal moments of the civil war, Lincoln's sense of the absurd would exhibit itself to the amazement of his staff. One time he called an emergency meeting of his cabinet to discuss the advances of the Confederate army into the North, and proceeded to recite passages from a book of humor while his staff sat there utterly flabbergasted. When he put the book down, he said, "Gentlemen, why don't you laugh? If I did not laugh I should die, and you need this medicine as much as I do."

DO UNTO OTHERS... Pattern breakers can also be wonderful for dealing with rejection. I decided to use a "pattern reversal" when I received one of many rejection notices for this book. (Mr. Davey served as my marketing rep for the book in New York)

Dear Mr. Davey:

Thank you for sending the proposal for the Terry Braverman manuscript. It is a charming collection but, regretfully, we have done so many similar works recently that we doubt that our list could sustain another one.

Sincerely,

Allan J. Wilson
Carol Publishing Group

I sent the following reply:

Dear Mr. Wilson:

Thank you for considering the proposal for Terry Braverman's manuscript. We appreciate your time in giving us a written response but, regretfully, we have received so many similar letters recently that we doubt Mr. Braverman could sustain himself through another one.

Sincerely,

Terry Braverman

LOOK ASKANCE. No matter how down or disturbed you may be, remind yourself to keep your ears peeled and your eyes pricked for pattern breakers in your environment (and in this sentence). There may be objects, people, situations or metaphors around you that are unusual, out of place or incongruous to the negative chatter going on in your head. Create incongruous scenes in your mind. How would it look if...

—Mother Teresa danced with the Rockettes?

—Jack Nicholson gave a sermon at your church?

—Woody Allen played Rhett Butler in a remake of *Gone With The Wind*?

Whether it's puzzling or amusing, allow the scene to disrupt negative thinking and shift you into a better mood. We can choose our state of mind. Life is a fantasy, made real by our thoughts!

PATTERN BREAKER REVIEW

- Alter your physiology (stand, run, shake, or do whatever it takes).
- Make silly sounds to release tension (grunt, bark, warble, squawk, chirp, oink, moo).
- Take different routes to work or to the store.
- Have breakfast for dinner, or dinner for breakfast.
- Eat a meal or brush your teeth with your opposite hand.
- Put on a clown nose and/or make funny faces in the mirror.

CHAPTER 4

RELENTLESS CHANGE IS TAKING ROOT
How To Be Flexible With Change

"If it doesn't work out the first time, you can make a sequel."
—Hollywood film director

After much redesigning, reorganizing, and restructuring, I changed my mind and decided to disband this chapter.

GOING WITH THE FLOW
A Brief Poetic Interlude

- Be willing to recreate, reinvent, or retool, even if it makes you look like a fool!

P.S. I have submitted this to the Guiness Book of Records as the shortest chapter in literary history—all may not be lost!

CHAPTER 5

JEST YOU & ME, BABE
How To Make Mirth With Your Mate

"Marriage is an ad-lib."—Steve Allen

The stereotypical relationship started in the Garden of Eden. After God served Adam and Eve an eviction notice from the Garden for eating the apple, the couple was forced to put on some clothes and look for another place. It was the turning point in male/female relations. Shortly afterward Eve turned to Adam, pointed at the crumpled old fig leaf he was wearing, and said, "You're taking me out in *that*?" Meanwhile, Adam had been standing around at the Garden exit gate for 2-1/2 hours, waiting for Eve to get ready. Thus began the challenges between men and women.

CLEAN FEAT. In a more contemporary scenario, Wendy looked at the floor and flew into a rage:

"I just finished vacuuming an hour ago," she fumed. "How many times do I have to tell you to wipe your feet before coming into the house?!"

Her boyfriend Richard, droopy and beagle-faced, muttered, "I'm sorry."

"Do you have any idea how frustrating that is?!" she snapped.

"All right, I'm sorry."

"You can be so unconscious sometimes."

"Look, I said I'm sorry!" His voice is rising. "How many times do I have to say I'm sorry?!" he thundered.

After a long pause, Wendy replied, "Four."

Richard chuckled. A whimsical smile had replaced his anger. He said, "OK, I'm sorry. That's number four, isn't it?"

They both giggled. End of argument, and a triumph of mirth over madness. Wendy's spontaneous humor in the heat of the moment prevented a minor conflict from becoming a major blowout. Her response to Richard's question elicited a shift from anger to amusement because it created a pattern breaker; thus, they were able to laugh at themselves and discharge the need to prove a point.

TUMS FOR THE TUMULTUOUS. It's a real discipline to have the presence of mind to access humor when we are engulfed by tension and tumult. An easy, effective technique for me in a standoff situation is when my partner or I say, "Stop the argument!" then proceed to put on clown noses and attempt to continue. Pretty difficult to maintain anger towards someone who has a red clown nose covering half their face! Or, rather than yelling at each other, try singing your argument in an operatic voice (more on that in the "Family Follies" chapter).

HONORABLE DISCHARGE. This is not to deny the importance of working out serious issues in a relationship, but rather to provide a way to break the downward spiral of anger, blame and shame, releasing the emotional charge of our position, and giving us a saner, more peaceful place to move into.

Discuss and establish with your partner if, when, and how it is appropriate to inject humor with each other in those trying times. The payoff is the realization of how insignificant most arguments are, and how a simple technique can return us to the joy of the relationship.

Finding humor in your relationships during arduous times can be like discovering gold beneath a pile of rubble. "We can be so heavy into proving ourselves. Humor can help us lighten up about ourselves and be less judgmental and self-righteous about others," said Dr. Susan Jeffers, author of *End The Struggle And Dance With Life.* "We have to stand back and be the observers of who we are by holding up the mirror, instead of putting the magnifying glass on our partner, and saying, 'Ah, there I am doing it again. Isn't that interesting?' Relationships are the greatest workshops going. They tell us what we need to work on in our lives. Seeing it that way makes it easier to laugh about our foibles, transcend our egos, and enter a state of love."

DOOR TO PERCEPTION. Several years ago I was involved with a woman who was very direct about what she wanted and finding out what I wanted in a relationship. In the beginning, she made it clear that she was not interested in having children and raising a family. This was good for me, because I wasn't either.

As our relationship grew her desires began to change, and six months later we had another conversation in which she revealed her longing to get married and raise a family, which was not in my game plan at that time. (I was still trying to release the notion that monogamy was a type of hardwood.) "If that is important for you now, then perhaps it would be best to stop seeing each other," I stated. It sounded good, but I was astonished when she agreed! Suddenly I was in a funk, and there was a long period of silence broken by a couple of questions:

"Do you want to go for a walk?" she asked.

"Nah," I mumbled.

"How about a movie?"

"Uh-uh. I feel like I want to go home and digest this."

I got up from the couch and shuffled to the door. She came to me as my hand searched for the doorknob and said, "I'm really sorry." I put on a veneer to the gloom I was feeling and replied, "Well, putting it in perspective, you get to move on and create what you want. I get to move on as well." I turned the knob to the left and pulled, then turned it to the right and pulled. Then I turned to her and said, "But it's damn hard to move on when you can't get the frigging door open!" In the midst of the pain, we both cracked up laughing, and we realized in that moment we could still have fun and be friends.

PRINCE OF PLAYFULNESS. In a survey of successfully married couples together for 15 or more years, the most important ingredient cited in their marriage was friendship: "My husband/wife and I are best friends." Second was mutual respect. Coming in third was, "My husband/wife and I laugh a lot and have fun together."

Even Walter Cronkite, when queried by a TV interviewer as to why his marriage has endured, responded by saying, "I think it's a sense of humor." And Walter isn't exactly known as the prince of playfulness!

A CHEEKY AFFAIR. My aunt Sarah and uncle Herbie have been married for over 40 years, and they're quite the funny birds. I worked up the audacity to ask my aunt if she ever had an affair or a one night stand the whole time she's been married to Herbie. As if on cue, uncle Herbie strutted into the room with a mock anticipatory look. To my surprise, Sarah answered the question. "About 30 years ago, I did have a one-night stand," she admitted. "But that was with Herbie." Their lovingly irreverent interactions make them fun to be around.

OIL THOSE SQUEAKY IRRITATIONS. "Are you upset with me because I came home late?" I asked my girlfriend. She shook her head no. "Is it because I didn't put away the dishes last night?" She said, "You have one more guess." I scratched my head to wake up my brain, and declared, "It's because I forgot to use deodorant today!" She made a buzzer-like sound and bellowed, "I'm sorry, but you do get the toaster and thanks for being on the show. I may not bring you back tomorrow as a contestant."

I laughed hysterically, and she smiled, as this little quip took the charge off her upset. We proceeded to tackle what was bothering her in a loving way. Remember—humor will not necessarily resolve an issue, but often it will act as a social lubricant to deal with issues more effectively.

THE IMPORTANCE OF BEING SILLY. I know a couple who has been married for 26 years, and they concur that a sense of humor is vital to the longevity of their relationship. I asked them, "Do you get to the point when almost anything your spouse does that used to annoy you just makes you laugh?" "Yeah, but it's not in the first couple of years," said Rob. His wife Janice added, "In addition to being funny, for us it's important to be silly. The world sees us as straight and reasonably dignified, and we're not at all dignified at home!" "We're able to come through a lot," concluded Rob. "Humor makes our flaws endearing, instead of annoying."

Finding humor in those perceived flaws can be pivotal in preserving balance. Does your husband hog the blanket in bed? Does your wife interrupt your conversation? Perhaps there is a silly code word or gesture you can create to neutralize those irksome quirks and share a laugh instead.

OUT-OF-POCKET EXPERIENCE. Another couple I know, Joanne and Paul, have been under financial stress. Nothing humorous about that, right? "There is value in everything," said Joanne, "and I've had to remind myself to let go of what I'm seeing. One way to do that is to lighten up. It isn't any big joke or any specific way, it's an awareness. We can still have fun, laugh, make love, take walks, and the financial stress doesn't become the all -pervasive emotional upset." When Joanne gets in a critical, moody mode, Paul will make a silly face or exaggerate her complaint, and she can't stay mad. A flexible perspective may not put money directly in their pocket, but it helps them stay levelheaded with the crisis at hand.

NO-FAULT ASSURANCE. A sensitive area in relationships is when we want to communicate our anger or discomfort with our partner's behavior to them, without hurting or offending. Let me indulge in having a little fun with the distinction between a criticism ("you" statements) and an observation ("I" statements):

"You scorched the meal!" (criticism)
"Honey, I saw some smoke billowing out of the oven." (observation)

"You're not wearing that tonight, are you?" (criticism)
"I detect an incredible radiance from you when you wear something else." (observation)

"Your breath is absolutely disgusting." (criticism)
"I notice how delicious your kisses are with an after-dinner mint in your mouth." (observation)

Humor delivers a great gift for us in the arena of criticism—the gift of having our mate be the reflection of our foibles and laughing at ourselves in the process, as opposed to taking it personally. What used to feel like criticism is transformed into something that lightens the heart and yet creates a deeper understanding of our connection to our partner, and others.

SEE NO EVIL. Another sensitive area in relationships is a roving eye. Let's face it—the desire for some men to turn and look at other women can be embarrassingly powerful. Even if I'm with someone with whom I am deeply in love, the impulse to just glance is still difficult to resist.

My girlfriend and I were at a party recently and I labored relentlessly not to notice a very attractive woman. Rather than "efforting," I opted to play with the urge. Whenever my girlfriend would look at me from across the room, I'd look up at the ceiling and whistle. Then she came over and said, "So, I see you noticed the sexy redhead." "The sexy who?" I asked. "Oh, come on, Terry. If she was standing there naked and her hair caught fire you wouldn't have noticed her, right?" "Who? Who?" I asked. "Hoo. Hoo," she replies, mocking me. "A wise owl you are," she quipped, with a hint of laughter. I smiled and looked up, starting to whistle again.

Situations that can be turned into running gags between you and your significant other can help defuse irritation over a wandering eye and other disagreeable behaviors. Humor can convert a disgruntled partner into a co-conspirator of amusement.

SLEEPLESS AND EMBATTLED. In the movie *The Prisoner Of Second Avenue*, neurotic New Yorkers Mel and Edna Edison (Jack Lemmon and Anne Bancroft) struggle to make their marriage work. Anxiety tears at Mel like a pit bull—he's afraid to tell his wife that he lost his job. He can't sleep, and the neighbors in the apartment next door are carrying on at 2 A.M. Mel presses his head against the wall, listening to the squeals of pleasure emanating from the other side:

Mel: Come here! Tell me you can't hear that.

Edna: Now I hear it.

Mel: Is it any wonder why I can't sleep?

Edna: Don't sleep with your head next to the wall. Sleep in the bedroom!

BEGGARS CAN BE CHOOSERS. While it's important to acknowledge the feelings of your partner, it also helps to keep complaints in perspective, as in this exchange with Marcia:

Marcia: I feel like I have to beg all the time to see you lately.

Me: It must feel that way to you. When have you felt that way?

Marcia: Well, uh....just before you left for your seminar in Hawaii.

Me: And before my East Coast trip too?

Marcia: No, I meant between your East Coast trip and your Hawaii trip.

Me: O.K. When else?

Marcia: Last night.

Me: Any other time? (silence) So, in the year and
        a half that we've been seeing each other,
        you've felt this way twice?

Marcia: (grinning) Gee, that isn't much, is it?

My intention was not to invalidate what she was feeling,
but to add some perspective. Sometimes we are prone to
exaggerate our grievances when we feel hurt or angry.
Putting our concerns in perspective with a humorous touch
can take the emotional charge away.

POSTCARD FROM THE EDGE. A major factor that
keeps long-term relationships fresh and stimulating is the
element of surprise. I believe this as much as anything will
create positive sparks and prevent the "automatic pilot"
syndrome from taking up permanent residence in your relationship.

You can generate surprise even when you're away from
each other. I recall a time when my significant other was
visiting relatives and vacationing in New York, so I sent her
a postcard from home (another pattern reversal). It had a
picture of the San Fernando Valley on the front (it never
looked better), and I wrote: "Hi honey, having a great time.
Weather's nice, wish you were here. Love, Terry." She
appreciated the reality twist, and felt all the more eager to
return home.

TRUE CONFESSION. A radical surprise is a powerful
device for affirming one's love for a mate. Recently my
girlfriend was ready to call it quits with me, citing over-

whelm with her business, uncertainty over her living situation, and feeling that perhaps we should just be friends. I felt very sad about this, yet I sensed there were other factors involved, either certain behaviors of mine that didn't sit well with her, or on a broader scale, she wasn't "getting" that my feelings for her were growing.

The next morning I determined to make a strong demonstration of love by showing up at her place early in the morning and telling her how I felt. I knocked hard on the door twice with no response. I proceeded to climb onto the rail in the front patio and hoisted myself up to the balcony, where there was a sliding door that opened into her bedroom. True to form, the door was cracked open, revealing my sleeping beauty. I tiptoed in and gently sat down next to her at the edge of the bed. She opened her eyes, not knowing what state she was in (dream or awakened), then affirmed the reality of my presence by touching my arm. Her face registered shock: "Terry! What..." I bent over and kissed her, and with a serious, determined demeanor I said, "I have some things I need to say..."

Lo and behold, she starts laughing hysterically! Talk about a pattern breaker—I must have looked like a beagle who just heard an eerie sound. Then she said, "Terry, I can't believe you did that, just walked right in..." With urgency, I declared, "Honey, I need to tell you some things." Still looking at me in shock, she said, "But I have to pee first."

I resigned myself to nature's call for her, knowing also that she needed to collect her thoughts over my sudden, unannounced appearance. When she returned, there was a warm glow in her eyes, a look that said, "I feel very loved."

The act of outrageous chivalry shifted the relationship to a deeper level of communication, caring and love.

NOTES OF ANTICIPATION. I relish playing hide and seek with my partner by tucking away little notes in various places. Once I stuck a note on the front door that read, "I just bought a terrific gift for you. Look in the jewelry box." There she discovered a message that said, "Couldn't fit it in the box. Check your green purse." When she looked in the green purse there was another note saying, "Sorry. It was too big for the green purse. Look in the pantry." There she encountered yet another note: "My apologies. It's too inti-mate for the pantry. Check under the bed sheets." Upon rolling back the bed sheets, she found a sexy nightie! The building of anticipation makes it all the more exciting.

PHOTO OP. Another time I was having a "wait" prob-lem in the supermarket checkout line, which drew my attention to a tabloid headline screaming at me from the rack. The headline read,

"Mom, 42, Hasn't Aged Since 18!" The subheading said, "She May Hold The Secret To Keep Us All Forever Young." Since it was my mate's 42nd birthday that day, I bought the publication and superimposed a photo of her over the photo of the woman next to the headline. It was a fun item to add to her birthday gift.

BACK SEAT DRIVERS. In his book *The Portable Romantic*, author Gregory J. P. Godek wrote this memo to Ford Motor Company:

On behalf of romantics everywhere I respectfully submit to you that your emphasis on aerodynamics and safety, while laudable, has been accomplished in part by the sacrifice in comfort and convenience of those who utilize automobiles for romantic activities. Must I spell it out? You have sacrificed copulatory comfort for fuel economy. It appears that automobile makers have lost touch with the people and the uses for which we purchase your products.

In the good old days, you may recall, motor carriages were roomy in order to accommodate the elaborate costumery of the day. Couples were able to stand upright while dressing or undressing—having, of course, drawn the curtains that were provided as standard equipment then. We, the romantics of America, call for the return of the roomy back seat.

Respectfully & Romantically Submitted,
Gregory J.P. Godek

One day I took my girlfriend car shopping and we couldn't make a deal with anyone; it was a bit frustrating. Later on that night we were sitting in the car in front of her place. She had hired a baby-sitter for her seven-year-old and wasn't due back until 10:30 P.M. Her place was a tiny studio, so there's no privacy from her child.

So here it was about 9:45 P.M. in a brightly lit parking lot and we were "making out" in the car. She felt obligated to go, but I reminded her that she could stay out until 10:30 and besides, the baby-sitter's ride wasn't coming before 10:30 anyway. I suggested that we park where it's dark and make love in the back seat. "That's crazy," she said. "It's so uncomfortable." I replied, "That's part of the fun. C'mon, it's a Saturday night." We got beyond our concerns as we rolled into the back seat, laughing a lot over the compressed surroundings—just like a couple of giddy teenagers again!

LIMITED ACCESS ROAD. The loss of spontaneity is a road to the relationship wrecking yard. When was the last time that you and your mate made love in the back seat of a car, broke out in a song or dance, romped on a deserted beach, or impulsively hopped into the car for a weekend getaway?

In the name of acting "responsible," we make lame excuses for curbing such spontaneous combustion. When doable, it is irresponsible to suppress those natural whimsical urges; throw your left brain out the window and go with the childlike creative impulses that bring so much shared joy among partners.

BOARDROOM ANTICS. My elfish, bearded friend Chas Eisner has a marvelous ritual he does with his wife of ten years. It's not an innately funny ritual, but it allows his marriage to maintain a certain levity, flexibility and understanding. On Sunday evenings, they get out of the home environment and sneak into an empty boardroom at a local hotel. They sit down with pad and pen, writing down any irritations, withheld communications, as well as acknowledgements and other subjects they had no time to discuss during the week. It's a great way to resolve issues and appreciate each other in a posh, neutral surrounding away from the distractions of home.

WHEN ROMANCE TURNS TO POOP. Have you ever gone to great pains to design an idyllic setting, only to find out your partner isn't in the mood? Mickey Chusid, another bearded friend of mine (I have so many bearded friends; why, I don't know) recently found himself in that situation. He wanted to surprise his wife when she came home from work, so he transformed the house into a romantic mecca. He filled the dining room, living room and bedroom with flowers. He graced each room with the soft, warm glow of candlelight. He donned his sexy, red silk kimono with the dragon embroidered on the back. Yes, he was breathing fire, and ready to sweep his woman off her feet.

When he heard the rumble of her car entering the driveway, his heart raced. His pulse quickened as her footsteps came closer. She entered, and as he approached her for the steamy embrace she said, "I've got to pee, then I've got to go to the store and get a pooper scooper for the cat. Do you want to come with me?" Well, all right. Sometimes this is what relationship is about. Our partner is not always on the same page as we are.

What to do with such disappointments? Build your mental muscles by pumping irony. The dichotomy in this case is so extreme that it is ripe for a humorous perspective. Set your mind on the irony of it. It takes discipline, it takes practice. She is where she is, you are where you are. The situation between these two could cause an earthquake or a "mirthquake." You have a choice.

MESSAGE FROM THE 'HOOD. Looking at an adverse situation with a shared sense of humor can take a relationship to the next level. A friend of mine kept getting the sense that it was time for him to find a new place to live. He and his girlfriend had discussed moving in together, but he was reluctant. Even though the large, two story town house he lived in was cozy, the street he called home was a daily overdose of noise—car alarms going off all hours, horns honking incessantly, and rowdy neighbors carrying on like lions in heat.

My friend did not act upon the feeling to move until early one morning when he shuffled out to his new car with his girlfriend and discovered that all the hubcaps were gone. For a moment, he had feelings of being violated by what happened; then he started laughing. His girlfriend was quite impressed with how he was handling it, and remarked, "You're taking this quite well. You've just been ripped off, and you're chuckling about it." He replied, "Well, first it's absurd that they would take only the hubcaps off a new car. And ultimately, I take this as a very clear message. It's time to get out of this neighborhood." He acted upon that message and immediately moved in with his girlfriend.

EGO MISSING IN ACTION. So how do you respond when the woman you deeply desire remarks, "I don't like the way you dress...I don't like the way you smell, and I'm not into the way you kiss." This is precisely what I was told by someone I was dating years ago. Although it sounds hurtful, it was said in a way that was not malicious; just gentle yet direct honesty. Still, I was absolutely floored, cowered, humbled.

Dress, smell....Well, I've been alerted to that by past girlfriends from time to time, but not liking the way I kiss...never! Intellectually, I said to myself, "Well, she must care enough about me to say such provocative things." But emotionally, physically, spiritually, I felt like dog poop.

To deal with it, I started to sensationalize the experience in my mind. I thought of a TV soundbyte from a network news anchor: "Mar Vista man's ego gets dismembered. Details at 11." I imagined a tabloid headline that blared:

MALE EGO GETS MUTILATED!
Grisly Phone Call Leaves Man Bloodied,
Yet He Miraculously Survives

One night I dined at a very elegant restaurant with the same woman. There was good news and bad news. The good news was she told me that I was everything she wanted in a man. The bad news was reaffirmed: "I'm not that sexually attracted to you." Not exactly music to my ears. How could this be possible? If I'm everything she wanted in a man, wouldn't the heat just naturally be there?

Shocked and dumbfounded, I called the waiter over and said, "I want to ask you a question. If you were with a woman who was everything you wanted in a woman, is there any way you would not be sexually attracted to her?" He looked at me quizzically and muttered, "Huh?" Realizing he didn't understand English too well, we laughed ourselves silly.

Special occasions are a perfect time to invent some fun with your loved one. Shortly after the aforementioned dining experience, it was Valentine's Day, and I decided to have a little fun with her complaints regarding my physical appearance. I bought a card that was blank inside and proceeded to print this on my computer:

VALENTINE CHECKLIST
CRITIQUE YOUR MATE

	Without a doubt	A little	No way
Dresses like alte cocker (old codger)	—	—	—
Smells like moldy bread	—	—	—
Kisses like dead sea bass	—	—	—
Chews food like rhino	—	—	—
Sleeps at rock concerts	—	—	—
Needs tummy tuck	—	—	—

I understand that one must be careful in choosing a lifelong mate. According to a recent study, 41% of all men don't wash their hands after using a public restroom. Fortunately, I'm not one of them.

LADIES AND GENTLEMEN.... Most men need to know that relationship is a process, not a result. Sometimes when a guy "gets" a woman, the tendency is to behave like, "Hey, I got the result. Now I can kick back." This "results" orientation makes women wonder why men don't profess their dying love anymore, don't bring home flowers, and just don't give as much loving care. Psst...hey guys, we need to keep stoking the fire with attention, affection, and acknowledgements—feed the relationship!

Some men have trouble with this because sometimes there is no immediate result, or we feel like it has to be something on a grand scale. We don't have to be Ben Hur riding into the bedroom with 40 chariots bringing up the rear. Doing the little things consistently, such as bringing flowers, cuddling and verbal expressions of love, will usually do just fine. And we don't have to do it perfectly.

Ladies, when your man does those little things, acknowledge him to the hilt. If you have any suggestions, save it for last, and do it gently. Some guys tend to have egos like balloons. An untimely criticism over something given to you, and the balloon bursts. The most common gripe for men: "No matter what I do, it isn't enough." Keep that in mind.

IDEAS OF SUSTENANCE. Monogamy does not have to mean monotony. For a change of pace, how about a romantic breakfast by candlelight? Get up just before dawn and welcome the day that way. Or both of you writing up a "joy" list—people, places and things that give you pleasure, satisfaction and fulfillment. Then share your lists with each other. Keep them around as a great reminder of what pleases your mate.

Get hold of a scene from a movie or a play, preferably a romantic comedy (e.g. a Woody Allen or Neil Simon creation), and read the script with your partner for fun. Really ham it up! Another fun, hammy idea comes from my friend Rina Daly. She makes a "date" with her mate to meet him at a nightclub, lounge, bookstore or coffeehouse. They travel separately, and when they encounter each other inside the establishment, he tries to pick her up, as if they'd never met before!

INVEST IN YOUR LOVE LIFE. Are you and your mate longing to get away from it all, but are saddled with an austere budget? Have a bowl, jar or basket at your bedside, and every time you make love, toss in a few bucks. I'd say fling in five, ten or twenty if you can. In a year's time, there should be enough for an opulent romantic weekend at least. If there isn't enough for bus fare, it's time to take stock of your love life!

As a form of "love maintenance," try sharing compliments and/or gifts with each other just before going to sleep. It is the time that your subconscious mind is the most receptive and will effectively reinforce the love in your relationship.

Better still, sing to your loved one as he/she is going to sleep, or when they open their eyes in the morning (assuming you don't have a voice that sounds like a garbage disposal). And guys, prepare a bubble bath for that woman of yours when she gets home from work after a hard day; ladies, give your guy a massage to soothe his cares away. Make a conscious, creative effort to break away from the same-old-same-old.

GIVE IT UP. What kind of choices can we make when we're angry with our mates? You can scream your lungs out until all your anger is released, or until your neighbors call the police. Or you can go to your cave to cool off and regroup. I'm going to make a very audacious suggestion for when you are angry with your mate: Sincerely give them something they will appreciate, like a gift. "After what he/she just did?!" It's a difficult feat because your emotions may be overwhelmingly against the idea, and your loved one may not want to accept the offering. Yet it is another means of injecting a pattern breaker to shift the emotions of both you and your mate, and return you both to a loving place.

There has to be some give and take in any relationship. Take artistic taste, for example. My girlfriend loves the French impressionists—Auguste Renoir, Claude Monet, Toulouse-Lautrec.... I prefer the modern impressionists— Rich Little, Dana Carvey, Robin Williams.... I buy her paintings, she buys me comedy tapes. Knowing our partner's preferences can save a lot of frustration and disappointment, and spare us from that pouty look of a kid who got all the wrong presents for Christmas.

TURN PAIN INTO PLAY. Dr. Annette Goodheart, a Santa Barbara, CA based psychotherapist, advocates laughter in her couples therapy. "Things get very serious between couples. The first thing I often tell people when they come in for therapy is, 'This really isn't serious.' At first they're stunned by that comment, then laughter frequently ensues.

"Seriousness is a tone, it's a way of relating to something. Although we don't always have control over what happens to us, we do have control and choice over how we relate to what happens to us. Charlie Chaplin's formula for laughter is to play with your pain, and that will trigger the laughter. If couples play with their pain and laugh together, they develop one of the top three characteristics found in most studies on long term successful relationships."

Playing with our pain and discomfort affords us the opportunity to reframe those touchy situations. Intimate relationships stir our deepest emotions, both positive and negative. Sometimes we get so caught up in the seriousness of working on the relationship that we forget about how and why it came together to begin with. Remember how exciting it was, and all the fun and frolic you had in the beginning? As it progresses, the superficial layers peel off, the communication gets closer to the bone, and the reality test sets in. It can get intensely heavy, but there is always another option. When you and your beloved are in a pickle, tickle the funny bone!

KEEPING THE FLAME LIT

- Exchange joy lists.
- Have breakfast by candlelight.
- Give your mate a gift when angry.
- Read a romantic comedy script with your partner.
- Put on clown noses in the middle of an argument.
- Compliment, acknowledge, and/or sing to your loved one at bedtime.
- Find a pleasant environment away from home to resolve issues, share appreciation.

CHAPTER 6

FAMILY FOLLIES
How To Put More Glee In The Family

"Before I got married I had six theories about raising children; now I have six children, and no theories."—Lord Rochester

George Burns once said, "Wouldn't we all like to say that we come from nice, loving, caring, close-knit families that live in another state?" Family matters can be trying, and moving to another state doesn't always help, but a state of humor will help us navigate through family favoritism, quirks, idiosyncrasies and upsets, and ultimately forge a path of love and understanding.

NON-TOXIC HUMOR. It is imperative that families engender a non-hurtful, connecting type of humor with their children that is inclusive, rather than a ridiculing style that can be so destructively alienating.

One of the most popular television sitcoms in history, *The Bill Cosby Show*, hired a Harvard child psychiatrist to screen all the scripts for derisive content. Says Dr. Annette Goodheart, "That's why after watching the show you not only laughed but you felt good about yourself, and felt better about your family, which is for many people a very different feeling from watching other family shows."

TEACH YOUR CHILDREN WELL. Humor is a powerful tool for teaching children. Researchers at San Diego State University studied the effect of humor and humorous examples upon the comprehension and retention of classroom material. Results indicated that although immediate comprehension was not facilitated by the use of humor, humorous examples related to the concepts in the lectures significantly improved retention of the lecture material six weeks later.

Humor is a powerful learning tool that provides true insight and reverses seemingly impossible situations. Parents, take note of this study—you will be more competent in disciplining your kids if you can find a way to make studying more fun.

In the movie *Stand & Deliver*, math teacher Jaime Escalante is confronted with a bristly, academically apathetic collection of students at an East L.A. high school—Hispanic kids who were dismissed as illiterate losers from disadvantaged backgrounds, with little hope for achievement in life.

Jaime was motivated to uplift his students into believing in themselves, but first he had to gain their trust. He did so by speaking their language and using humor. He made friends with them, drove them home, sat down and ate with them. He got in their heads. He got to know their families and implored them to take a more active role in their childrens' education.

The first day of class, one of his students said, "Can't we discuss sex?" Jaime remarked, "If we discuss sex, I would have to give sex for homework." The classroom exploded into laughter. The next day he was dressed like a chef, and taught them fractions by placing apples that were partially sliced, some in halves, some in quarters, on their desks.

With wit, tough love, perseverance, and enlisting the support of the parents, Jaime guided his students to unimagined heights of achievement when they all passed the Advanced Placement Calculus Exam, a test that a mere 2% of all California high school students had passed the previous year.

MIRTH MASTERS. Children can be great teachers too. Their sense of play is infectious and reminds us grown ups of the need to put more fun and spontaneity in daily living. They ask funny questions and make amusing observations that you can share at cocktail parties. They make funny faces at you, hug and kiss you at a moment's notice, or jump into bed and playfully roll around with you, in a way that can brighten up a bad day. They can even make you laugh when you're angry with them, hastening the lesson of forgiveness.

SCRAMBLED EASY. The language of little ones is a never ending source of amusement. Kids create a "scrambled eggs" type vocabulary that is unique and often funny. My friend Michael's six-year-old daughter likes listening to the "radio-do-do," she likes to eat "avocado-do," when she has a cold and her dad teases her with jokes, and she says, "Dad, you better stop that or I'm going to break out in coughter! Your jokes are very nervigating."

PULSATING BEAT. Comedian Steve Allen's oldest son, who is a doctor, has a four-year-old son. "One day he was lying on his dad's chest, when suddenly he lifts his arm and whacks his dad real hard across the chest. It was startling and dad angrily said to his little boy, 'Andy, why did you do that?' In all seriousness, Andy replied, 'I wasn't getting a pulse.' Jayne and I sometimes use that line when one is not getting a response from the other."

THE MAIN EVENT. A friend of mine, Dr. A. Jayne Major, is the founder of the Parent Connection, Inc., a company that helps to improve family relationships. She told me, "One of the things our family did at the dinner table was an MSE, or most significant event that occurred that day. It was a great way to touch bases with everyone. It wasn't always funny, but the potential was always there."

FUN & GAMES. Getting kids to complete domestic tasks can be a challenge. Whether it's doing dishes or screwing in a light bulb, making it more fun will make it more palatable. My friend Liz and her three kids, ages five, six and eight, make up silly songs while doing chores. My friends Ben and Brenda play rhyming and word association games with their little ones to keep them amused while they clean their room. For her teens, my masseuse friend Michelle plays rock music while they tidy up the house.

HOME ALONE. Whether it's a night out on the town or an extended business trip, leaving your child for any length of time may be hard for them, particularly if they are in their "clingy" phase. Give them a cassette tape of you singing a silly song or reading a funny story while you're away. Leave notes that take them on a treasure hunt, leading to their favorite treat. Have your child start a scrapbook of all their favorite things to do, favorite foods and people, pictures of him or her, school awards, etc.

If you're going away for a while, pull out a map and mark with them where you'll be; have them highlight your route, stick pins in places you'll be staying and when you'll be there so they can have fun tracking your trip.

ROAD RAP. When you are traveling with kids, getting to your destination on time is generally not an option, yet the most common phrase uttered on family trips is, "Are we there yet?" Bathroom breaks and growling stomachs make it seem like you're traveling by rickshaw.

Occupy your little ones' minds with word games, e.g., what vegetable looks like a tree? Or, what can you spread on toast that rhymes with ham? Create silly stories by each person adding a word to it. Bring scripts from popular children's movies and have them each take a role—most kids are naturally hammy.

In his book *Here's Looking At You Kids,* Hugh O'Neill has some cheeky travel tips for parents:

- Throw out your maps. If it's before noon and the sun's on your right you're headed straight for Santa's workshop. That's all you need to know.
- Don't even think about your actual destination, just think about the terrain that will get you there. If you're heading from Cleveland to Woonsocket, don't focus on Rhode Island but on the farmland of western New York that is your path east.

- Carry the legal limit of apple juice. Take out the spare tire and pack the wheel well with those boxes of juice that come individually wrapped with little tiny straws. The downside of a flat in February on a highway outside Bozeman, Montana, is no big deal compared to a drink drought on a sunny day in Palm Springs.
- Never give Aunt Nancy and Uncle Bill an even vaguely precise time of arrival. They will only start worrying if you're a half hour late. In a perfect world you shouldn't even tell them you're coming. But if you feel you must offer an exact time of arrival, choose one from the following list:
  A. By the next full moon
  B. During the next administration in Washington
  C. In time for the new millennium

DRIVING MOM UP A TREE. I recall when my mother took me out to the country for my first driving lesson, on a hot summer day. Negotiating my way down country lanes was a snap until I ventured to make my first parallel parking attempt. Mom was nervous about it, and rightfully so—I backed the car into a tree. Before she had a chance to "go off" on me, I quickly said, "Gee, it's a nice day to be in the shade, isn't it?"

CHEER OF THE UNKNOWN. My mother has been driving a 1977 Dodge for years. When I visited her recently, she expressed an interest in getting a new car. So we went to a dealership and she wanted to test drive a particular model. She was at a loss when she got behind the wheel—for her, it was like driving a space shuttle, with all this strange gadgetry she was unaccustomed to. Firing up the engine hasn't changed, but to get her old Dodge in gear you pull down on the stick that protrudes from the steering wheel. On the new vehicle, she pulled down on that stick and the wipers came on! We were all convulsing with laughter, including mom. I think it helped her to relax with the unfamiliarity of driving a new car and enabled her to enjoy the smoother ride. Next lesson: teaching her how to record on the VCR.

NOISE POLLUTION. My mother lives in New York ('til death do they part), and doesn't believe the world really exists beyond New Jersey. She loves the city and when I last visited her, I advocated taking a short trip to the country for quiet and solitude. She retorted, "It's too noisy out there!" I said, "Too noisy in the country?" She declared, "Yes! Those crickets would drive me crazy!"

Mom is also very creative at devising ways to lure me into staying with her for a visit. Here are some of the classics:

"My car won't start."
"I can't get my VCR to record."
"There's a big sale at Bloomingdale's."
"The Ice Capades are closing next week."
"You'll have to see this new blender I just bought."

QUEEN OF DE NIAL. On a recent visit to New York, my mother reminded me of an incident from childhood, when my brother and I went on a rampage for the 4th of July. We were nine and ten, and running up and down the street throwing cherry bombs (explosive fire crackers) down the sewers. Later that evening, while we were upstairs in our room, we heard the door bell ring. It was the police! They informed my mother of reports about our mischievous activity, which mom vehemently denied: "That's impossible. My boys would never do anything like that!"

Meanwhile, my brother and I were hiding in the closet, shaking in our shoes, worried about being taken away. Later that night, she questioned us about it. Our response was, "Mom, we would never do anything like that!" When I was 40 years old, we were reminiscing one day and she brought up the incident again: "Did you and your brother really do that?" My response: "Mom, we would never do anything like that!" She said with a smirk, "Uh-huh. I thought so." Laughing at our transgressions doesn't make them right, but it allows forgiveness to soothe those grating family matters.

LEAVE A MESSAGE. Mom doesn't always feel appreciated for her good deeds. She was starting to feel that way the last time I stayed with her. I was sitting at the kitchen table with my suitcase upright on the floor next to me. I just finished using her telephone and placed it on top of my suitcase. She came over to me and, pointing a finger directly where the telephone was, said peevishly, "I want you to know that I washed out some underwear and a pair of pants for you and put it in there." I followed her finger and replied, "You put it... in the phone?" Now, I knew she meant the suitcase, but my quirky perspective of noticing the phone right there created a moment of humor that allowed both of us to laugh and lighten up.

Humor is probably more responsible for developing a close relationship with my mother than anything else. Laughing with each other helps us accept our idiosyncrasies and heal old issues.

FOOD FOR THOUGHT. Do not underestimate the use of pattern breakers for defusing family spats. My brother and I were embarking on a heated discussion by phone recently, and when he was about to escalate his tirade I strongly blurted out, "Hamburger!" There was a stunned pause on the other end of the line, then, "Huh?" I said, "You mentioned you were hungry for a hamburger, so let's meet at a restaurant in 15 minutes." It immediately derailed the argument, and when we met for a meal we both forgot about our trivial disagreement entirely.

Does your family obsess over food? God forbid if any of my relatives got into an auto accident. Instead of paramedics, they'd call in a team of caterers: "His collarbone is broken! Give him a chopped liver sandwich with a side of pickles." My grandfather would always goad me with the standard routine, "C'mon, eat. Food is a terrible thing to waste. You hardly touched your plate. What's the matter, you don't feel well?" This was after I'd already had three servings of everything. I would feel guilty if I didn't inhale every single crumb on my plate.

Eating is certainly an activity that can bring families together (at least logistically). Rather than having it be a mechanical exercise in "empty calories," why not create some mirth around the dinner table? Dr. Annette Goodheart encourages her clients to have "finger food evenings" where families put a sheet of plastic under the table and play with the food, eating and feeding each other with their fingers. Imagine doing that with rice, peas or mashed potatoes!

As a kid, I had a passion for peanut butter and jelly sandwiches. I must have had it for lunch every day for ten years. I ate it every which way too—I grilled it in butter in a frying pan, I baked it with bananas, ate it cold the next day. It infiltrated my clothes, hair and facial pores.

If your child is a one note samba when it comes to food, strike up a restaurant style menu in advance for all three meals with several choices for each meal. Make it fun by allowing him or her to order from the menu selections.

MELODIC MEDIATION. When I began giving workshops in 1988, I created an exercise called "Sing Out Your Stress," in which anyone who cared to and dared to could come up to the front of the room and sing a personally stressful event in any musical style.

A friend of mine has used this technique with his girlfriend's 13-year-old and 11-year-old. Whenever they are squabbling, he has them sing it in an operatic voice. "It's so funny to watch them singing opera: 'You left your dirty underwear on my bed!' countered by a twittery falsetto, 'No I didn't, no I didn't.' They find it funny too, and it usually will defuse the argument."

As an addendum, a nurse I know makes her kids go into the shower stall when they're arguing to pacify the little combatants. And if you're not quite ready for singing out your disputes, try bickering in a foreign language, or complete gibberish, and take turns.

I once again verified the usefulness of this approach in a recent workshop, when I asked the group if anyone had a stressful event that week. A 13-year-old boy raised his hand and came to the front of the room. I requested that he sing out his experience in an operatic voice. It was initially trying because he kept laughing at the thought of it. Finally, he composed himself and sang an aria about how mad his mother was when he didn't finish his homework. After the last note, he limply collapsed on the floor, convulsing in laughter, and the whole group howled with him.

OUT OF THIS WORLD. We've all heard stories about people who have had contact with aliens, yet I've never seen any. Have you? I have a theory about this: I believe that most aliens have assumed the bodies of teenagers.

Think about it. They don't act like us, dress like us, or talk like us. Their rooms will sometimes have an orderly quality, like a trailer park after a tornado. When they sit down at the dining table, it may look like a crazed rock band at a ballet. Sometimes their dinner table discussions include aesthetic, cerebral topics like slugs mating, frying ants in the sun with a magnifying glass, or the size and color of elephant poop.

Two Sentences You May Never Hear From Teenagers:

1. "You're right, mom."
2. "You're right, dad."

The teens are probably the toughest transitional years there are. Although it is tempting to tease teenagers about their ways, it is generally not advisable. Much sensitivity underlies their search for identity. Sharing fun activities and directing humor at yourself is the best approach.

Remember that we were all teenagers at one time. With teenagers, be patient before you become a patient!

"Walter, I want you to have a talk with your son-- he's got a job, his own apartment, he doesn't borrow money-- I mean, it's just not *normal,* for crying out loud!"

GRAND FINALE. Grandparents will often anchor a family with their patience, wisdom and wit. A friend told me about his 103-year-old grandfather who lived his twilight years at a retirement home. "My grandfather liked to poke fun at himself. He would joke about his age, saying that he hadn't seen a movie since *Birth Of A Nation* debuted. He was also a life-long smoker. One day I came to see him and brought a carton of cigarettes. He said, 'I think that maybe I should stop smoking.' I asked him why, and he replied, 'I just read it causes cancer.' "

FAMILY COUNSELING

- Favor inclusive humor over ridicule.
- Enjoy the silly language of your kids.
- Have finger food meals with the whole family.
- Invite family members to sing when they argue, and while doing chores.

CHAPTER 7

YOUR MONEY OR YOUR LAUGH
How To Get Funny With Your Money

"A journey of a thousand miles starts with a credit card."
—Michael Horn

How cheerful and relaxed are you when it comes to money? As my friend Michael Horn would say, "Are you wondering if there's life after debt? Do people refer to you as King Cashuncommon?" Are you on a steady diet of budget cutlets? Would Publishers Clearing House send you a rubber check, if you won their sweepstakes?

When the going gets tough around money, a merry heart will guide you through and beyond the maze of old beliefs about struggle, lack and limitation. It can be hysterically funny how worried, attached and obsessed we get with our money!

Jack Benny, the acknowledged king of the tightwads, satirized this brilliantly in a sketch that had him being held up at gunpoint. When the gunman says menacingly, "Your money, or your life!" Jack strikes his patented pose, pondering the choice, and says, "I'm thinking..." In real life, Jack was reputed to be a generous man; making fun of the tightwad persona reminds us all to lighten up our relationship with money.

MONEY TALKS. If your money could communicate to you, what would it say? "Darling, take me out before I get old and wrinkled," Or conversely, "You don't give me a moment's rest! I feel wasted." Would your money say, "You just don't appreciate me. I feed you, clothe you, give you a comfortable home and a car, and you treat me like dirt. I'm outta here!" Or, "Do you want me locked up in a safe all day? You're too possessive with me! I need to go out and circulate." Money is like any other form of energy—it is meant to circulate.

Of course, it helps to be prudent for deciding how to circulate your money. From the book, *Accent On Humor*: "Last week I spent $400 to fly to Florida, $100 to rent a car, $30 for gas to drive to a $150 a day resort to attend a $395 seminar called *Money Isn't Everything."*

Prosperity is a state of mind. If you can see, hear, touch, taste and smell, you're conscious of prosperity! Being alive is a sensual banquet. But if you're saying, "I still don't have enough money," what's enough? If you're not sure, check the following lists.

You Have Enough Money If You...
—fly to Paris for dessert
—pay cash for a skyscraper

—water your lawn with Evian

—use Tiffany lamps for tanning purposes

—polish your floor with Estee Lauder's private collection cream

You Don't Have Enough Money If...

—toothpicks are a luxury item

—you sleep on an ironing board

—you heat your food by candlelight

—your goldfish eat more than you do

—you keep all your money in a pillbox

"Having enough" is a very relative concept. Millionaires have a lot of money in most people's eyes, yet some of them are chronically worried about money, while some of the poorest rejoice in what little they have and feel as though all their needs are being met. While observing the demeanor of two men, Ben Franklin said, "Mr. Parsons, even in prosperity, always fretting. Mr. Potts, in the midst of poverty, ever laughing. It seems then, that happiness in this life rather depends on internals than externals..."

Whether we have a lot of money or not, true prosperity resides in the joy within us. In his book *Everyday Wisdom*, Dr. Wayne Dyer says, "The first step towards discarding a scarcity mentality involves giving thanks for everything that you are and everything that you have."

So what does humor-associated laughter have to do with money? It keeps us in balance when we undergo financial setbacks. It keeps the little voice of fear out of our ear. Fear is the major block to attracting money. Fear and mirthful laughter cannot co-exist!

When we are in a mirthful state of mind, our energy level is high. Energy attracts more energy, and money is a form of energy. Creative ideas start to flow. When we are amused, our minds are stimulated and we don't get fatigued so easily.

COLD CASH NO MORE. Boosting your "amuse" system will keep you from levying a stranglehold on your money and inhibiting your enjoyment of it. History has its share of eccentric people in that regard.

There was a story about a woman who made millions in the days of the California Gold Rush, and kept every cent of her money on her person, for fear of losing it. One night, she got drunk and stuck all her money in the stove. Later that night, it got quite cold. She lit the stove, and all her money went up in smoke!

LAUGHING STOCK MARKET. In the documentary film *Marx Brothers In A Nutshell,* writer Norman Krasna reflects on an encounter with Groucho: "One afternoon in 1929 Groucho lost $230,000 in the stock market. Years later, he took me to the VIP gallery at the stock exchange. At the top of his lungs in a vaudeville voice, he starts to sing 'When Irish Eyes Are Smiling.' The whole stock exchange froze like a painting. He sang two lines, then stopped and said, 'Fellas, I lost $230,000 here one Friday afternoon in 1929. I am now going to sing two choruses of 'When Irish Eyes Are Smiling.' And he started again.

"Now, the (ticker) tape is coming in blank all over the world. They must think there's an earthquake in New York. So Groucho finishes the song and everyone gives him a tremendous hand. He looks down to the floor and says, 'Don't just stand there, you could be wiping someone out in Beverly Hills,' and does five minutes of shtik. They were roaring at every joke, and the stock market went up several points that day. I don't see why they didn't keep Groucho there permanently."

STRANGER INTERLUDES. A joyful heart is an open heart, open to both giving and receiving. Become equally great at both, and be outrageous in your giving! Next time you're at a toll booth on a highway, pay for the person behind you—it's worth it just to see the look on their face as they pass. Pay for the person in line behind you at the movie theater. If he/she asks why, say that you may never see them again, and wanted to part amicably. Notice their reaction.

Tip someone who normally doesn't get a tip. So what if they're strangers? As my friend Peter Rosen once said, "Strangers are just friends who haven't yet met." You may meet a new friend, lover or business partner this way. It will make you feel totally abundant, and the feeling may attract more money to you.

FUN RAISING. Another gem from the book *Accent On Humor*: "Andrew Carnegie was a charitable man, but he also believed that people should work for what they got. After seven years as the sole supporter of his local symphony orchestra, Carnegie decided that it was time for the fundraisers to earn their keep. 'You will no longer get your total budget from me,' he told the stunned representatives. 'I will contribute only an amount equal to the donations you get from other sources.'

"The fundraisers departed in shock. But two days later, they returned with half the symphony's budget, $3.5 million, already pledged. Carnegie was greatly pleased. 'I hope this teaches you young fellows a lesson,' he said as he wrote out a check for $3.5 million. 'Surely two days was not an unreasonable investment of your time and efforts. May I ask where you raised such a large amount in so little time?' The head of the fund raising delegation smiled. He said, 'We got it from Mrs. Carnegie.' "

I strongly recommend donating to whatever or whomever feeds your soul (church, organization, etc.), no matter how much or how little money you have. I've had a lot of resistance to giving money in the past, and some of my classic excuses included:

—I'm sick
—I'm tired
—I'm broke
—It's tax time
—It's taxi time
—I gave last week
—I gave at the office
—I gave enough already
—My car is double parked
—I have to go to the bathroom
—I left my checkbook at home
—I have to take my poodle to the vet

Give something even when times are tough. Practice the law of circulation. If water doesn't circulate, it becomes stagnant. If blood doesn't circulate, the body will suffocate from lack of oxygen and nutrients. Even a small act of giving affirms a sense of abundance within you.

Giving is an act of faith that will ultimately find its way back to you in some form or another. It is not, however, about getting brownie points from a Higher Power! God doesn't hang out counting the donations and declaring, "This soul gave a bundle, I'll give him a palace in my Kingdom," or "This one only gave a dollar, I'll give her a closet in the Kingdom, but nothing more." Give from your heart.

"I take as my text this morning line 34b of form 1040, which deals with charitable contributions."

DANCING IN THE STREET. The universe will let you know when it's giving time. One time a big, burly homeless man came up to me on the street and asked, "Can you spare me some money?" I replied, "How much?" The man asked me for a couple dollars, and I gave it to him.

The man clutched the money in the palm of his hand and gazed at it for a moment. Then suddenly, it was as if the clock had struck midnight on New Year's Eve. He lunged toward me with a huge bear hug, and was jumping up and down with glee. "Praise God, praise God!" he shrieked. "Say it with me!" Caught up in his excitement, I joined him in saying, "Praise God, praise God!"

There we were, dancing around on a busy downtown street in L.A. It looked like an epileptic form of ballet, I'm sure. When we finally stopped, the man said, "Thank you brother." I responded with, "My pleasure. Thanks for the dance." We headed off in opposite directions.

About half-way down the block, I heard a shout: "Hey!!" I turned around, and the man was standing there, giving me the thumbs up sign. The medium of exchange turned into an extra large exchange of energy. Remember— money is energy. The fun we get from playing with it is what we're after!

Know that when we're out to do the world good, then the world is out to do us good. It's called cause and effect. This will open us up to receive. A lot of people have not been open to receive, due to childhood conditioning. Perhaps some of us were told that it is better to give than to receive by someone who was receiving. Accept everything that comes your way gleefully, no matter how large or small the denomination.

Affirm that money comes to you in all forms, in all ways. If you happen to see a coin lying in the street, pick it up. It's yours. Even if it's a penny—if you leave it there, you're sending the wrong message to the universe by pushing it away. Affirm that it is a part of your good fortune.

FAUX PAS DE DEUX. Author and seminar leader Stuart Wilde is one of the great proponents of accepting all monies coming your way, no matter how minute. This hilarious story is from his book, *The Trick to Money is Having Some*: "In London I was entertaining a group of VIPs from the U.S. I had decided to take them to the ballet at the Royal Opera House, Convent Garden.... I had bought a Rolls and hired a chauffeur to get around the transport problem. I had arranged for the driver, Slick Vic we called him, to wait at the curb directly outside the Opera House so that at the end of the performance I could whisk my guests off to dinner.

"As we came out of the Opera House, crowds milling, distinguished guests in tow, I began to cross the sidewalk to the car. There to the left was a penny. It had been raining so the penny glistened, reflecting the street lights and the shadows of those lights, flickering as they did through the crowd, giving the impression that the coin was in fact winking, taunting me to walk past it. I hesitated, wondering what everyone would think as I groped around at their feet. Then I decided that an affirmation is an affirmation so I went for the penny.

"What should have been a graceful scoop turned into a fiasco. I hit the penny with my knuckles and it began a long loping run across the sidewalk, snaking in and around many an expensive shoe. Determined as I was, I refused to give up. I lunged at the itinerant coin and missed, ending up on all fours. God knows why I had chosen to wear a white satin suit that night. By the time I had the penny in hand I had also acquired the muddy water on the sidewalk.

"Meanwhile, Slick Vic had ushered my guests into the car, and they observed my adventure with restrained astonishment. I was really embarrassed and felt I had to offer an explanation. So I told my American friends that the penny routine was an ancient British custom that brought untold amounts of good fortune.

"They were fascinated and one of them even began taking notes. When pressed as to exactly how the 'penny in the gutter' routine entered British folklore, I told them it was a custom handed down from Elizabethan times, and before long I named Queen Elizabeth, Lord Dudley and Sir Walter Raleigh as those who crawled across the floor of Hampton Court in chase of the Royal Penny.

"I must say that secretly I felt proud of myself. From time to time I opened my hand to glimpse the great yet muddy prize, while I mused that there is no limit to abundance when you are committed to going for it."

AROMATHERAPY. A French king had a court jester known as Jehan. Some jesters were prized for their wit and wisdom by their Royal Highnesses, and one day Jehan was asked to act as a judge in Paris. A greedy baker had sued a poor man for sitting outside his shop. "I had only dry bread to eat," the poor man explained. "I sat outside the shop because the smell of the food cooking inside seemed to make my bread more appetizing." "He ought to pay me for the smell of my food," the baker argued. "Of course he ought," Jehan agreed. He ordered the poor man to rattle some coins in his pocket. "Do you hear that clinking?" Jehan asked the baker, then adding, "That's your payment. The *sound* of the money is paying for the *smell* of the food."

A SIMPLE GENIUS. At one of his "Rich On Any Income" workshops, financial coach Rennie Gabriel met a lady who had a mentally retarded cousin. While her cousin was employable, having an IQ in the low 80s, he could only get jobs paying minimum wage. At a young age he was trained to pay himself the first 20% of any income he earned, and after handling obligations like rent, food, etc., he could spend the rest on whatever he wanted.

Because he always paid himself first and was retarded, he did not think of any excuses, justifications, or create a clever way to avoid doing what he was trained to do with money. Despite working low-paying jobs, by the time he was in his 30's he had saved over $100,000. Perhaps some of us are too "clever" to save money.

NET MIRTH. Rennie also told me about a doctor who came to his office. He was single, did not own a home, and made $165,000 per year. Asked to list where his money went, he could only think of three places—rent, car payment and auto insurance.

When they totaled up everything he owned and subtracted everything he owed, he had a negative net worth of

$20,000. In conclusion, my friend told him, "Based on your income and my expert advice, with proper planning you'll be worth nothing in less than six months (and that would be an improvement)."

GENERIC HUMOR. Try having some playful adventures with money. My friend Terry Mullery recently told me a story about someone who was at a supermarket, loading up his cart with generic items, such as "Beans," "Beer," "Soap," etc. While on line at the checkout, he took out a piece of paper the size of a check and wrote the word "Money" on it.

When the cashier had checked his items, he handed that piece of paper to her. She was completely befuddled. Her jaw hung open and she mumbled, "I've never seen this before." She got on the microphone and said, "Store manager to checkstand two." The store manager came over, saw all the generic brands being purchased, then saw the "generic check" and, laughing hysterically, took out his pen and wrote VOID on the check.

Embracing the fool within can reap positive rewards. It makes risk taking more fun. This is good, since there is often an element of risk in creating more money. The fool within can jump outside the normal constraints of convention, shed new light on old problems, and inspire creativity. According to the *Encyclopedia Of Tarot Cards*, by Stuart R. Kaplan, "The fool card can signify enthusiasm, initiative, spontaneity, new adventures, opportunities and possibilities."

Humor can come from the tiniest places. A man who was dining in a Chinese restaurant cracked opened his fortune cookie. The message said, "Gold is in your future." Ironically, he was a stockbroker who trades in metals!

In the Bible, God says, "Go forth, produce and multiply." This marked the beginning of network marketing. Of course, this quote can apply to anything, from making pots to making love. As you go forth to realize your dreams, remember this: Everything is on loan from our abundant universe, and God has easy terms—enjoy it while you have it, and use it joyfully.

LIFE ON LAYAWAY. People with prosperity consciousness will probably live longer. However, there may be drawbacks. George Burns, who was a wonderful example of how mirth can keep us on earth for a long time, relates this story about a neighborhood doctor: "Dr. Stern was a very considerate man. He gave one of his patients six months to live, and when he found out the patient couldn't pay his bill, he gave him another six months to live."

Why is humor such an essential ingredient to enjoying money? **Perspective**. On our road to achieving our financial goals, we will go through variable speed zones, detours, new construction, signs (watch for those), moments of feeling lost and times when we need to check the map. Humor allows us to detach from the challenges we face and gives us the courage to carry on.

Perhaps you will also need a financial guru. I have one for you. His name is Swami Investananda. The Swami used to run a Jewish deli, when his name was Harry Krishner. Harry had the best smoked salmon in town. One year, he and his salmon made centerfold for *Field & Stream* magazine.

He did well financially, but wasn't really happy until he discovered his calling. So he started a new religion called Hinjewism. Devout Hinjews believe that all life is not only sacred, but profitable!

Swami suggests that you invest in the following companies:

Sasha's Psychic Roofing Service
—leaks repaired psychically
—no house calls required
—unconditional three lifetime warranty

The Astral Travel Agency
—many planes to choose from
—leave your baggage behind
—no guilt trips

Take the Swami's advice—stop worrying about money! Save and invest. Save funny cartoons, quotes and one liners. Invest in a humor library, toys, games, and a clown nose. Fatten your portfolio in mutual fun. Swami Investananda can be reached at 1-800-GET-GELT.

COLLECTING MONEASE

- Create a funny currency or check.
- Pick up any unclaimed coinage lying around.
- Give to whatever or whomever feeds your soul.
- Pay for a stranger (bridge toll, on line for a movie).

CHAPTER 8

HUMOR CAN GIVE YOU THE BUSINESS
How To Succeed In Business Without Really Frying

"Columbus did not know where he was going. When he got back, he didn't know where he had been. And he did it all on borrowed money. There's hope for all of us."—bumper sticker

"We want to have fun!" is how Herb Kelleher, CEO of Southwest Airlines, sums up his corporate philosophy. Chronic seriousness that characterizes many corporate cultures gets lost in a maze of mirth at Southwest. Kelleher has been known to feed peanuts to startled passengers aboard flights, and show up at a Southwest hangar in a flowered hat and a purple dress at 2 A.M.

Prospective employees are asked to write a joke on their job application, watch a company video of briefcase-toting pilots dancing off a plane to rap music, and flight attendants wearing wild costumes and even singing the in-flight instructions to passengers.

JOVIAL SECURITY. In-flight frivolity by Southwest pilots and flight attendants entertain the passengers and alleviate "cabin pressure." One pilot airs the sound of a train whistle when preparing for departure. A flight attendant goes through the safety regulations ritual with lines like this: "There may be 50 ways to leave your lover, but there's only six ways to leave the aircraft...," or (after the plane has taken off), "This is a non-smoking flight. If you wish to smoke, please step outside the cabin."

Another flight attendant, when confronted with hungry, impatient travelers who get pretzels instead of a full meal, jokingly remarks, "I'm putting all of you on diets for this flight." She concludes, "Humor is the biggest thing that keeps me going. It really helps."

A ticket counter agent finds humor useful in defusing tension with chafing passengers. When they feel anxious or irritable about catching their flight, she'll cheerfully say things like, "Don't worry. They're all waiting for you." She's amazed that some people take it literally. They respond by saying, "Really?" and think they're receiving special attention. "The other ones who pick up on the light-hearted cheekiness will usually manage a faint smile. But it's all in how you say it," she adds.

Doesn't all that merriment get in the way of the bottom line, considering the tough business climate of the airline industry? Not at all. In fact, Southwest is the only airline that has turned a profit every year since its third year. It has the lowest turnover of personnel, least amount of sick days taken by employees, and, according to Department of Transportation Consumer Reports, the fewest customer complaints, best baggage handling and best on time flight record in the industry.

JEST MANAGING. Richard Cronin, a management consultant, once surveyed 737 company executives. He found that 97% agreed that a sense of humor is a determining factor in hiring personnel, and 60% felt that a sense of humor can be a key element that influences how successful a person is in the business world. In another survey conducted by Burke Marketing Research, 84% of the personnel directors who were interviewed said that employees with a sense of humor do better work.

We tend to make mistakes when we are uptight. W. Edwards Deming, the father of total quality management, said the most important thing managers can do for their company is "drive out fear."

Fear of making miscues inhibits creativity and productivity. Humor helps to overcome this fear and let go of feeling shame when we do mess up. One way you can help alleviate someone's anguish is to gather a group of co-workers and give that person a standing ovation when they walk into a room. Watch their face light up!

TURN IN THE DIRECTION OF THE SKID. In the business world, the wheels of change are burning rubber. A permanent job has become an oxymoron. The business world is in a state of constant flux and turmoil. Once-potent corporate giants are staggering around on a lean diet to survive. Companies synonymous with gold watches and large pension funds are either laying off thousands of people, being bought out or disappearing from the corporate landscape.

Due to rapid changes in technology, restructuring, and global competition, you can't rely upon the status quo. Vir-

tually all of us will be between jobs or businesses, perhaps
frequently, during our work lives. We need to continuously
recreate and reinvent ourselves and our skills. It is important to detach our sense of self-worth from transitional circumstances and maintain perspective on who we are by
enhancing our sense of "self-mirth."

After recent layoffs at the U.S. Robotics West Coast
HQ, the remaining employees lived in constant fear
wondering who would be terminated next.

CORPORATE VOODOO. Companies in transition like to rotate buzzwords to describe the same predicaments. A friend of mine works for a large defense contractor, and four years ago he said the company was going through a major "reorganizing." When I saw him a year later he said the company was "restructuring." How is that different from reorganizing, I wondered. "Phase two. New level of reorganizing," my friend said. The following year he asserted that the company was "redesigning." I assumed this was a more stylish version of restructuring, emanating from the evolved management practices that originated in reorganizing.

Last year, he proclaimed at a recent networking event that the company was now "reengineering." Changing letterheads, painting the lunchroom, even cleaning out one's desk qualifies as "reengineering." The bathroom on the third floor had a sign on the door that said, "Closed for Reengineering." Everything in the company is being reengineered, from the cooking utensils in the cafeteria to the CEO's wardrobe. Use your imagination to invent your own buzzword for various tasks you do.

With corporate takeovers, mergers and acquisitions running amok, imagine this as a future headline in our daily newspapers:

RUPERT MURDOCH ACQUIRES THE CATHOLIC CHURCH

ROME. At a press conference today in St. Peter's Square, the Vatican announced that Rupert Murdoch will acquire the Roman Catholic Church in exchange for common stock shares in his media empire. If the deal is approved, it will be the first time a media mogul has acquired a major world religion. Pope John Paul II will become Senior Vice President of the company's new Religion Division. "We anticipate tremendous growth in the religious telecommunications market in the next decade," said Mr. Murdoch. "The additional resources of the Catholic Church will allow us to make religion easier and more accessible for a wider audience of people. Through our telecommunications systems, we will make the sacraments available via satellite for the first time...through new interactive media, you can confess your sins, obtain absolution, and reduce your time in purgatory, all without leaving the comfort of your own home." Mr. Murdoch said he intends to give the church a racier look for wider public appeal.

What's going on at your place of work that is major news? Create an amusing headline and story, and share it with your staff. Instead of being traumatized, dramatize it with humor.

"Go away, Mr. Turner. We've already merged with News Corp."

TECHNOFROLIC. As if mergers, acquisitions, and constantly changing markets aren't enough to deal with, businesses are having to master new technologies that could be obsolete within months, or even weeks. Lack of familiarity with new equipment can make people loony, but can also lead to funny interactions. Mark Darby, a registered nurse from Omaha, shared this rib tickler: "A lady came to the hospital to visit a friend. She had not been in a hospital for several years and felt very ignorant with the new technologies. A technician followed her into the elevator, wheeling a large machine with tubes and wires and dials and lights that she thought was a ventilator. 'Boy, I would hate to be hooked up to that thing,' she said. 'So would I,' replied the technician. 'It's a floor cleaning machine.' "

The incessant relearning that results from changing technologies can cause your brain's hard drive to crash. I remember when I upgraded to my current computer with all the bells and whistles. There was so much to learn it was intimidating, and I approached it with all the confidence of an amateur prize fighter stepping into the ring with a heavyweight champ. So I gave my computer a name—I called it "Schmegegi" (the Yiddish word for clown). I put little furry creatures on top of it. Create some humor for yourself by personalizing new equipment, putting your favorite toys, props, or pasting cartoons on them.

FRISKY MANAGEMENT STRATEGIES. Bringing laughter and appropriate play into the workplace is the quickest path to building camaraderie and teamwork. There are numerous ideas for contests that can be implemented. A team at one company had everyone bring in photos of themselves when they were babies, and held a "cutest baby" contest.

Another company had a "silly hat" contest, while another created a "worst hairdo" day. Pick up some wild props at your local toy store or novelty shop and keep them in your desk. Pull them out when timely to puncture tension and remind others to lighten up.

One manager periodically emerges from his office striking a mock authoritarian pose and cracking a bullwhip. Keep in mind that it is important to strike a balance between the task at hand and the need for "social orientation."

TAMING CIVIL UNREST. If your business happens to get its share of difficult customers, and it is taking a toll on employee morale, you may want to render a version of what one bank called its "Worst Customer Story of the Week Award." This bank was beset by low morale among the tellers, who constantly complained about troublesome customers. So every Friday the teller who had the best (most horrific) story about a difficult customer won a bottle of champagne. It improved morale and increased customer satisfaction because tellers were now seeking out those hard-to-please patrons to win the award. Customers responded by becoming more civil, as a result of the increased attention.

OBJECTIONS SUSTAINED. Customer relations can certainly be a challenge. If you or your company has made a mistake, you might want to try this one on a frustrated customer: "We've been in business a long time. We must be getting a bit senile." When I gave my humor workshop for a company that needed help in customer relations, that quip was a big hit!

If someone is so blatantly hostile and nothing comes to mind that is witty, simply say, "Thanks, I guess I needed that." Instead of getting reactive and defensive, you go with it and redirect the energy in a way that can be disarming.

REDUCE TENSION, GAIN ATTENTION. A little clowning around relaxes me when I'm under stress in business situations. I remember the first meeting I had with a corporate officer to propose a seminar. He was a regional vice-president for one of the nation's largest banks. When approaching the towering building that was their headquarters, I started to get nervous. I always carry a clown nose in the car, and pondered wearing it into the building. "Too inappropriate," barked my logical mind. "Ah, but you're shaky," implored the clown within. Besides, the red colored nose coordinated well with the gray suit and subtle red stripes. The clown won.

I sauntered into the skyscraper with an air of dignity. The security guard said, "Good morning," initially looking stunned, then grinned ear to ear. I'm getting loose. I am waiting for the elevator with three Japanese businessmen, who are gawking at me like I'm one of a rare species from the Amazon jungle. As we board the elevator, I decided to have fun with them. "I bet you're wondering why I have this nose on. You see, I have double vision, and I have a tendency to walk into walls and doors." I demonstrated by bumping into the elevator door with my nose as we were ascending. "This helps to cushion the blow." They looked at me and smiled politely, nodding their heads.

When I got off the elevator, I chuckled at the thought of their bewilderment, and imagined them conversing about the incident on their flight back to Tokyo. By the time I entered the meeting, I was relaxed and effectively sold the VP on my program.

AN EDUCATED MESS. According to a recent study, people who have a lot of personal power are perceived as being expansive, casual and relaxed. Executives need to be skillful at reframing situations that are challenging, and transforming them into new possibilities.

There's a story told about Tom Watson, the founder of IBM. One of his subordinates had made a terrible mistake that cost the company ten million dollars. He was called into Watson's office and said, "I suppose you want my resignation." Mr. Watson replied, "Are you kidding? We just spent ten million dollars educating you."

SHOOTING THE BULL. Merrill Lynch's CEO, Dan Tully, asserts a flamboyant, extroverted approach to the stodgy world of finance. He welcomes friends and customers alike with a broad comic brogue and has been known to croon "Danny Boy" to a roomful of brokers. Tully also wears corny neckties and likes to hand out tiny lapel pins depicting the Merrill Lynch bull to everyone from clerks to finance ministers. While Schwab and Fidelity may corner the market on media ink, Merrill Lynch is quietly thriving under the colorful leadership of Dan Tully.

LIFE AFTER DEBT. A lighter touch can increase business success in the most serious of matters, such as collections. In 1992, when the country was mired in a recession, I met a man on a cross-country flight who was the head of a collection agency. I listened to his tales of woe and frustration over the pile of outstanding accounts. I asked him if he could show me a copy of the letter his company sends out for collection. It was typically heavy-handed in substance. I suggested he try forwarding letters with funny relevant quotes or cartoons.

He thought I was crazy, and I wasn't so sure if I was or not, but we had plenty of flight time left so we brainstormed a few ideas. As we parted company I doubted he would use any of them, but three months later I received a surprise call from him, and he was excited. He used some of the quotes and cartoons; collections increased by 15%!

CHOIR PRACTICE. An employee at a local department store found a fun-filled answer to the problem of learning new company guidelines for clerks. She's also an aspiring singer, and with management's blessing, created a "compliance choir" who sang the new guidelines over the store's sound system just prior to opening the store. The tune was not only catchy, but the clerks caught the message as well, and fewer mistakes were made during new policy changes.

Studies have shown that a humorous approach can improve memory. For example, if you take your daily to-do list and weave the items together in an amusing way, perhaps as a visualization or funny story, it will be easier to remember all the things on your list.

Much resistance can show up when implementing new company guidelines and policies, blocking retention of information. One time I was hired to announce a company's new safety regulations as several of the celebrity characters that I do. This not only entertained and disarmed the disgruntled staff, but it proved to be effective in helping employees retain the new information, because they connected it to the "celebrity characters" who said it.

A VARIETY SHOW. How else can the show biz approach be implemented in a training environment? We know that it is essential to entertain while teaching, so what other talents can be employed? In addition to singing and impersonating (how about doing The Godfather leading a sensitivity training?), can you draw or paint something, do a magic trick or card trick, juggle or dance, or dress in accordance to the theme, to illustrate a point?

One particular CEO is also a ventriloquist, and brings his dummy to board meetings, especially when there is unpalatable news to serve up. It seems to make it more digestible when it comes through the dummy (which one, you ask). Board members say that it helps to cushion the blow, causes chuckles and inspires creative options.

Be creative and have fun in the way you present ideas and material to staff. Remember—if you're in management and/or training, you're in show biz!

GAME SHOWS HIT THE JACKPOT. In *The Laugh Connection* newsletter, humorist Bob Ross elaborates on how one company boosted their bottom line through fun and games. After several years of using the obligatory pie charts and overhead projectors to stoke productivity and customer satisfaction, employees responded with suppressed yawns and no results. Meetings were as exciting as a leaky faucet, so management solicited the aid of employees to spiff up the process.

A committee of employees were formed to produce "Zero Defects Day" meetings, with the condition that they stay within the budget. They made their debut with a spoof from the TV game show *Wheel Of Fortune*. It featured a manager in the role of TV host Pat Sajak and another bearded employee wearing a wig and a gown as Vanna White. Each committee member had a role, from announcer to cameraman to producer.

After the usual presentation of facts and figures, the show began. Other employees participated too, and later gave the meeting rave reviews. Responses transformed from "Oh no, not another ZD Day," to "I wonder what they're up to next quarter" (perhaps a mustached female employee doing *Jeopardy*'s Alex Trebek).

You might ask, "What is so effective about a couple of guys impersonating game show hosts?" The meeting was a success in building employee morale by promoting fun, creativity and spotlighting hidden talents. Co-workers began to see each other in a new light, with renewed respect and camaraderie.

More parodies of TV shows ensued. In order to empha- size the cost of mistakes in manufacturing, they produced a game show called, "The Cost Is Right," where contestants guessed the cost of specific defects in their manufacturing process. That was followed by "Foundry Feud," which challenged participants to answer questions about quality awareness.

Management found that the show biz approach was effectively communicating messages about quality, which was a great improvement over the old style "Sominex" meetings. The payoff—after five years, late delivery was reduced by 40%, returns from one division were reduced by 85%, defects in one area were cut by 77%, and delayed shipping had fallen by 85%.

SELLING IN STYLE. At IBM, Inside Sales Executive Karen Donnalley oversees a staff of telemarketers who sell computers nationwide. Servicing about 75,000 accounts "is a very difficult job," she acknowledged. "It's really important to recognize even the small successes in this environment. I try to make sure my team is happy. People who like their job do a better job."

Ms. Donnalley's mirthful management approach has not only achieved great success for her department but has also given her wide acclaim as an innovator in the company. "It's really good to laugh at yourself too. Sometimes I'll have the management team do funny things. I'll say to someone, 'You're in charge of morale this week. What are you going to do?' For one of my birthdays, they built me a throne, handed me a cape and I was crowned 'Queen for a Day.' "

In Donnalley's work world, some mornings have been started with the chaotic din contrived by musically hapless salespeople on drums, tuba, accordion, and other instruments played in a mini concert. A gong is hit when a salesperson closes their first deal of the day, and they advance a wooden horse bearing their photo down a racetrack. She's initiated a crazy socks day, a silly hat day, and organizes monthly skits ranging from presidential debates to nostalgic dress up themes. "There are thousands of people in this building complex who will all be abuzz about it. People that we've never seen before will come up to our floor, just to see what's going on. But we have to stay fresh. Every idea we have can't be used all the time."

Donnalley believes that if her staff is feeling good, it's projected in the phone calls to customers and makes them feel good. A happy customer translates into more business. In one year, her department's sales increased by 30%, and in six months her staff grew by 50%. "It's very much about business commitment. I have my strong side too, but being able to laugh at myself and with my team has brought a loyalty and dedication that I treasure. It keeps people wanting to come to work." And keeps other department heads calling her, wanting to know what she's concocting next.

A BANKABLE STAR. There are embarrassing moments that may be tough to live down, especially if you're a banking rep. A networking associate shared this story about a former colleague: "An associate of mine went out to see a client after taking over the banking relationship for the company, and her first meeting was with the CFO. The CFO was taking her on a tour of the corporate offices and he said to her, 'Cheryl, I need to show you the president's office because it's so elegant, comfortable and has many amenities.' She said, 'Well, maybe we shouldn't disturb him.' The CFO replied, 'It's no problem. He's not in yet.'

"They ambled in and she was very impressed by the posh surroundings. Now at ease, she eagerly inquired about seeing some of the amenities the CFO mentioned. So he walks her around the corner to the president's own private washroom, pushes the door open and there was the president of the company, sitting on the throne! He looked at her and said very sheepishly, 'It's nice to meet you. I don't know who you are, but give me a few minutes and I'll be right with you.' There must be something to exposing yourself—they proceeded to strike up a very cordial business relationship."

DOUBLE VISION. Language snafus can be a great source of humor in business. Chuck was a salesperson for a car dealership. A short, big-eyed woman with a duck-like gait approached him and said she wanted a two door car. Her accent was thick and she had only lived in America for a short time. Chuck showed her a two door car and the woman blurted out in a shrill voice, "But I want two doors." Chuck was stunned. "This is a two door," he retorted. The woman shook her head and said, "No, two doors each side."

PATERNAL AGREEMENT. To be effective in negotiations, it is said, one needs to maintain an emotional detachment from the interaction. This story of a management-labor contract meeting comes from the book *In The Presence Of Humor*, by Cy Eberhart:

"One of the management negotiators explained that tensions were rising as they broke for lunch. Upon leaving the conference room he was handed an urgent message to call home. He called his wife and tensed up when he heard her distraught voice, but then relaxed in amusement when she described her concern. The school principal wanted to meet with her about an incident regarding their son. She was upset over what might happen. He told her over the phone that nothing terrible would happen and gave her some tips on how to handle the meeting with the principal.

"Returning from the lunch break, he was still amused by his wife's reaction to the school 'crisis.' He appeared even more detached from the intensity of the negotiations. The others, alert to his behavior, wanted an explanation. He said it was just a personal matter that had nothing to do with the negotiations. But they insisted on knowing what was going on, so he told them. They all laughed and got back to business.

"The seemingly impossible then occurred. With an ease and quickness that startled him, they found areas of agreement and made remarkable progress. Before lunch, he had been a person 'on the other side.' In telling his story, the others understood because they were husbands and fathers too. When the negotiations resumed, it came from a solid base of commonality rather than differences."

BATHROOM HUMOR. David Lewis, a Los Angeles attorney, shared a story of how humor defused a tense moment in negotiating for the purchase of a large office building. "The negotiations were going on very hard, night and day, and one night it got to one of those tense moments when two of the guys on opposite sides of the table were arguing about the height requirement for the urinals in the men's room. One of the guys was insisting it was 30 inches, and the other guy screaming no, it's 36 inches.They were really going at it, and I jumped in and said, 'Gentlemen, I think we're in danger of getting into a pissing contest.'

"It broke the tension and really resolved the whole situation. Everybody relaxed and we moved into a place of equanimity. They realized it didn't make any difference anyway."

A FORD-ABLE DECISION. An injection of absurdity at staff meetings can be used to effectively make a point. In his book *What They Don't Teach You At Harvard Business School*, Mark McCormick gives an example: "Many years ago, the Ford Motor Company went through a period in which the numbers people (accountants) took over the company and were closing plants left and right in order to cut costs. They had already succeeded in shutting down plants in Massachusetts and Texas and seemed to be relishing their newly found power.

"Robert McNamara, who was president of Ford at the time, called a meeting of his top executives to discuss a recommendation he had received for the closing of yet another plant. Everyone was against it, but the predictions from the accountants were so grim that nobody was willing to speak up.

"Finally, a salty Ford veteran by the name of Charlie Beacham said, 'Why don't we close down all the plants and then we'll really start to save money?' Everyone cracked up. The decision was made to postpone any more closings for a while, and the bean counters went back to working for the company instead of running it."

Humor levels the playing field. A shared laugh makes all the participants realize there is a common thread running through all of us. They all agreed that something was funny, and in that moment the possibility opened up for them to agree upon other things. This is why humor can be so valuable at meetings. It reminds us of our common heritage, otherwise known as our humanity.

UNDERWEAR AND TEAR. There may be times when it's inappropriate to inject humor in those circumstances. You can still access humor without saying anything. In a television interview, I was once asked how a person can keep their cool during intense negotiations when others are getting so testy. I replied, "Just visualize them wearing polka dot boxer shorts." I have visualized people who were yelling in my face in their underwear, wearing a diaper, or wearing nothing, and it definitely helps to take the charge off the encounter.

THE DREAM TEAM. Humor can be a terrific builder of teamwork. My friend Tom Daly gave a seminar on teamwork in which he facilitated a particularly fun and revealing exercise (created by his wife, Rina, a particularly fun and revealing fact).

He took me and seven other volunteers from the group to the back of the room and instructed us: "When I say, 'GO!' I want one leader to stand in the middle, and the rest of you to lock arms with each other in any way you choose around the leader. Then, in collaboration with the leader, you're going to move this small folding table with the tray on top (and a coffee mug on top of that) from one corner of the room to another." I immediately had a vision of how it could be done quickly, and when Tom asked us how much time we needed, I said we could do it in two minutes.

When Tom gave the signal to proceed, I jumped in the middle and asked everyone to lock arms and face me, except for the person closest to the table, who I had turn to the outside of the circle and lock arms with the rest of us. He asked me if one person could carry the whole table and I said, "Yes, absolutely! You can do it." With little time for processing, I had to be assertive and think fast to get the job done in two minutes.

We proceeded to move en masse toward our goal. Everyone else was laughing as we shuffled across the room and down the aisle, with the guy toting the table bringing up the rear. Then an obstacle showed up in the form of an overturned chair in our path. Before I could give an instruction, the person at the front of the circle kicked the chair aside. "Good job, macho man!" I shrieked, which provoked more laughter from the rest of the room. We got to the corner and I told the team to rotate so that the person with the table would be facing the corner. Then he set the table down, and the task was finished in a minute and twenty seconds.

This humorous exercise was a great learning experience for all of us. Tom asked me my thoughts about leading the group. I replied that I probably would not have led if not for the clear vision I had for getting it done simply and quickly. I mentioned that in the limited time frame of two minutes, it didn't occur to me in the heat of the moment that the person carrying the table was walking backward! I could have rotated the team at the start so he would be walking forward, but the chair in the aisle may have been a bigger problem.

Each person on the team gave their viewpoint from the questions Tom asked of them: Did they feel like an integral part of the team, even though they had no verbal input? One person suggested it was easier to yield to the strategy given by the leader and work with a team of strangers than her co-workers (perhaps knowing their flaws all too well and the personality dynamics between them). Were any of them tempted to dispute the leader's strategy? A few were, but said they ceded to the leader due to time limitations. Was it fun? Unanimously, a good time was had by all!

CORPORATE GIBBERISH. A manufacturing company in Oregon lightens up their corporate office by compiling outrageous and nonsensical phrases and bloopers, spoken and written at company meetings and seminars, called "Job Related Gibberish." Some examples are as follows:

"Born again feedback"
"Contaminated criteria"
"Jurassic parking policy"
"Process-oriented lunch breaks"
"Well constructed orifice memos"
"Organic team conception at birth"
"Monitored objective evaluation observed"
"Prioritizing the concept of self-extermination"
"Interfacing pluralism with a diversity assortment"
"Well calibrated collection of unencumbered gender models"

In the Monkey Business World

GRIN AND AIR IT. Notice the common denominator in all of the examples of humor in the workplace mentioned in this chapter—humor as a shared experience, not directed at anyone. This brand of humor creates a common perspective that allows for improved interaction and greater productivity. It is a very effective use of humor in the business environment.

If you are going to poke fun at someone, let it be you, or a person with whom you have a solid relationship and you know they will take it in good humor. This is especially true if the humor has a sarcastic twinge to it. Otherwise, I would definitely avoid sarcasm or any humor that is at someone else's expense.

Poking fun at yourself is a safe form of humor, unless you bludgeon yourself with it, which makes others uncomfortable. If you're doing business in Japan, it would be wise to avoid self-deprecating humor—it's not OK in their culture. On the other hand, they love puns and cartoons. Neutral subjects such as the weather are usually OK to make a joke of in any culture. Common gripes that a group of workers share collectively are a safe haven for humor. But no matter what, there is always an element of risk involved because you cannot be absolutely certain how people will take it.

Humor can fall flat and even boomerang, depending on the mood, the timing and the environment. Keep those factors in mind and use your intuition. If you are uncertain at all, you can preface your remarks by saying, "I just thought of something that I think is humorous. Can I share it with you?" Even if it flops, at least you had their permission to share it.

MAKE IT RELEVANT. Recently I was at the California Gift Show, having a discussion with someone about giving humorous, novelty or gag gifts to corporate clients and staff. "There's a lot less of that type of thing than there used to be, because of that 'schlock' factor," said Patti Cohane, editorial consultant for a publication called *Gift & Stationery Business.* "People have to make a distinction between what's tacky and what's tasteful. Rather than just indiscriminately buying anything, make it relevant with a current theme. Give it to staff people as a way of saying, 'you've really done a good job,' or use it to cheer someone up who is having a bad day."

As we read at the beginning of the Family Follies chapter about inserting humor that is pertinent to the subject matter being taught, so it is with using relevant humor in the corporate world.

MEMO MADNESS. A shared sense of joy and fun helps to promote trust, teamwork and creativity in the workplace. At a recent seminar I gave in Hawaii, participants were given a typically heavy-handed memo from a hypothetical company to rewrite in a humorous fashion. I had them break off into teams of six or seven people to brainstorm funny, creative and outrageous ideas.

It proved tremendously valuable in terms of people laughing and creating together. After allowing them about 20 minutes to recreate the memo, each group appointed a spokesperson to read their revised versions to the rest of the group. I was amazed at how clever most of them were (and the participants were impressed with their own humor and creativity). One woman in particular had all of us in stitches—she read her team's memo in Hawaiian pidgin English!

A human resources director I know uses humor to make sure his memos are noticed. Whenever he has an important memo to send to other departments, he will attach it to a little toy or prop. That way, the memo will not only get read but will be remembered as well. If the memo conveys bad news, it can take some of the sting from it.

OTHER MIRTHFUL MEMOS. "The Board of Directors commissioned a panel to form a committee to study the review of this year's recycling program."

This memo comes from a major real estate company:

Memorandum To: Glendale staff

Subject: Sam Conley

CORRECTION

After Sam's surgery he will be recuperating on a beach in Puerto Vallarta drinking rum punches for two months, not two weeks. Sam will be away from the office starting Monday, January 27.

As promised, Sam will keep us informed with daily updates on the tanning process relative to the type of rum consumed.

VIOLATORS WILL BE TRESPASSED. Change can not only be unsettling, but downright chaotic. At Huntington Memorial Hospital in Pasadena, CA, a shortage of parking spaces had developed. After months of meetings to tackle the problem, administration revealed plans for a new parking structure. However, precious parking spaces had temporarily vanished while construction took place, and the parking lots were knotted every morning. In this submission from the book *Making Humor Work*, by Terry Paulson, Huntington's personnel manager showed how to defuse some of the frustration in the following memo:

To: Employees
From: Management
Re: Employee Parking Rules

Employees may participate in a demolition derby that starts in employee parking lots each morning promptly at 9:00 a.m. after all the spaces are filled. Employees who do not participate will automatically be declared losers. Employees who park illegally one time will be warned, after two times, will be stripped and flogged in front of other violators, and after three times, will be forced to eat all their meals in the employee cafeteria. Employees whose cars stick out in traffic lanes will have their rear ends painted red. If they continue to park that way, we will do the same thing to their cars.

BUDGET CUTLETS. Budget cutting can send a shiver down the spines of company employees; when taken to a level of absurdity, it can be quite amusing. From the movie *The Prisoner Of Second Avenue*:

Secretary: I put some vouchers on your desk to sign.

Mel: For what?

Secretary: Sandwiches sent out for yesterday. From now on, no outside food can be charged to the company. It was an egg salad and a Coke, wasn't it?

Mel: Yeah. And a pickle. A big pickle.

Secretary: I included the pickle.

Mel: Good. I don't want to cause any concern at the stockholder's meeting.

DUDE FOR A VACATION. It's important to reassess our careers when we have time off from our jobs and businesses. Is it time for a change, or do we simply shift our perspective regarding our work? In the movie *City Slickers,* Billy Crystal plays Mitch, an overworked, disillusioned radio ad salesperson who acts upon a lifelong fantasy—taking a vacation at a Western dude ranch to experience cowboy freedom with his close buddies.

At first, he agonizes over making the decision to go, with all the responsibilities of a heavy workload and family tugging at him. But his wife urges him to do it, saying that recovering a sense of aliveness and a sense of humor was more important than anything else at that moment.

As the film progresses, Mitch discovers the value of laughter and living life as an adventure. Upon his return from the Wild West, nothing in his life has changed outwardly: He still has the same job, the same family, the same problems. But having rediscovered his smile enables him to embrace the same circumstances of life with a new perspective and a renewed sense of joy.

OPPORTUNITYISNOWHERE. This header is actually a sentence. Depending on how you look at it, the sentence says, "Opportunity is nowhere," or "Opportunity is now here." Your perspective can be your biggest ally, or greatest enemy.

NETWORK LITE. Times have changed. Business used to be strictly about closing deals; now people talk about "nurturing their network." It's more like breast-feeding than browbeating. Business has a softer, more fluid aspect to it, with emphasis on building relationships and injecting more fun.

In Los Angeles, I belong to a business networking group known as the All Cities Resource Group, composed chiefly of bankers, attorneys and CPAs. This is a group I would have avoided for most of my life, fearing that I might contract a case of chronic seriousness from them. But if you came to one of the group's meetings, you would have a howling good time.

The camaraderie, triggered by the sometimes raucous humor and laughter, may be the main reason why a lot of business is transacted. The members are very competent professionals who happen to take themselves lightly. The group certainly lives up to its motto as being "the fun place to do business."

ACCEPTING RIDES FROM FRIENDS. There are many of us who are seeking to capitalize on new business opportunities, from network marketing to the Internet. How many of you have been contacted by an old friend you haven't heard from in ages, who enthusiastically says, "I have this exciting opportunity I want to share with you!"

Before you tell them that dinner is on the table, they launch into a ten minute hyperbolic promotional pitch.

Some of these opportunities are great, yet it's easy to fall prey to soaring expectations of untold riches instantly gratified. Maintaining enthusiasm and taking consistent action during the brick-by-brick building of a business, with all its trials and tribulations, is a challenge. Add a generous helping of humor to go with persistence—you will need it. An old Chinese proverb said, "He who waits for roast duck to fly into mouth must wait very, very long time." We must learn to laugh at our mistakes—there may be lots to laugh about!

SOUND BUSINESS ADVICE

- Poke fun at yourself first.
- Employ talents for training purposes.
- Give awards for worst customer stories.
- Keep a few toys and props around the office.
- Create funny headlines and stories for major changes.
- Compile and post outrageous and nonsensical jargon.
- Do game show spoofs to test new skills and knowledge.
- Form a compliance choir to teach new guidelines, regulations, etc.
- Personalize new equipment by naming it and pasting cartoons on it.

Doug now realized that he never should've fallen
asleep before take-off.

CHAPTER 9

LIGHTENING UP YOUR LOAD
ON THE ROAD
How To Travel "Lightly"

"Thanks to the interstate highway system, it is now possible to travel across the country from coast to coast without seeing anything."—Charles Kuralt

Since we are such a mobile society and spend so much time commuting and traveling in our motorized contraptions, I felt compelled to write a chapter on staying light while in transit. Flight delays, language barriers, accommodation snafus, and hindrances from local authorities can foil itineraries and challenge our sense of composure.

ARRESTED FOR MIMICKING CELEBRITIES. One time I was driving through a ghost town in Arizona when a highway patrolman pulled me over for speeding. If an alien wanted to know what a highway patrolman was like, here was the perfect prototype—a burly man with a face that resembled that of a Great Dane.

He was about to write me a ticket when he noticed that I lived in L.A., and asked me what kind of work I did. I told him I was a recovering stand up comedian who gave seminars on humor and how to lighten up. He smiled and said, "That's pretty interesting." After a short pause I said, "Could you use some of that down at the station?" He burst out laughing, shook his head, and replied, "You know, I'm gonna cut you some slack this time. But you have to come down to the station and give us your best celebrity impressions." I agreed, and instead of giving me a speeding ticket, he wrote up a warning ticket and wished me a nice day when I left the station.

COMEDIC JUSTICE. Veteran stand-up comic Conrad Lawrence is a self-described "road dog," a man who has plied his trade from town to town for over 18 years. He has never missed a gig. "I've been through hurricanes, tornado alerts, hailstorms, blizzards.... One time I broke down in the middle of nowhere in Alabama...I had a Dodge van, and I blew a tire. It was off the main road and pitch black outside, so I got my flashlight out and put on a spare tire. I was hauling butt down the road, going about 80, and was stopped by a cop right before I got into town. I said, 'Officer, you can arrest me or do whatever you want, but I've got a gig in about 10 minutes. I'm a standup comic and...' He cut me short and said, 'Oh, you doin' the comedy tonight over at the Razzle Dazzle?' 'Yeah.' The officer said, 'Follow me.'

"He escorts me to the club with siren blaring and the light twirling atop his police vehicle. When he got out of his car, he came over to me and said, 'If you ain't on the list, you're goin' to jail.' In fact, he stayed for the entire show. Afterwards, he approached me and started writing out a ticket. I said, 'Oh man, are you going to give me a ticket?' He looked at me and replied, 'Here. It's called a freebie. You only get one in this town.' He actually wrote on the ticket, 'freebie.' "

Humor has a way of cutting through the roles we play and creates rapport. Law officers deal with a lot of difficult people and stressful situations. If you can jest during arrest, you just may get off lightly.

IDENTITY CRISIS. If you are a well-known celebrity, there are disadvantages to being recognized wherever you go. But what if you're a celebrity not recognized and need to pass inspection? Steve Allen recalled such an incident. "One time I walked up to the security desk at the State Department in Washington, where I was late for a meeting. The man said, 'And you are...' obviously not recognizing me. So I said, 'Steve Hitler.' He wrote it on the visitor's badge and said, 'Here you are, Mr. Hitler. It's on the third floor to the left, second door.' "

FLUSH AND BLUSH. Sometimes situations can be funny and potentially dangerous. I was on my way to an out-of-town gig one day when it felt like my bladder would explode any minute. I couldn't wait much longer and pulled off the freeway in search of the nearest restroom. There was a five story building immediately on my right with a flag in front. As I drove up I saw a couple young girls, perhaps 10 or 11 years old, in uniforms exiting from the building. Assuming it to be a private school, I ignored thoughts of me being an intruder and entered the school.

My timing was perfect because the lobby area was devoid of people. I approached the men's room and, alas, there was an "Out of Order" sign on the door, and the door was locked. But I was a man on a mission, and had no intention of leaving without relieving. I marched across the lobby to the ladies' room, and knocked on the door, then carefully cracked it open and warbled, "Is anyone in here?" Whew, no answer! I helped myself to a stall and happily proceeded to lighten my load in tranquility, when a loud bell went off to signal a change of classes.

Suddenly, the bathroom was besieged by a flock of young girls! Oh well, just hang tight for a few minutes, I figured, and they'll be off to their next class. I'm amused by the situation, but...uh-oh. Five minutes goes by, then ten minutes, and they're still yacking away with their girl talk, a steady stream of them coming in, going out, coming in.... What's going on? I cued in to the conversation and discovered they were readying themselves for a class photo session. Oh God. Fifteen minutes elapses. I hear one of them say, "Is someone in there? Someone's been in that stall for an awfully long time." She taps on the stall door and says, "Is someone there? Are you OK?" "Yes," I respond in a Julia Child-like voice. Time is ticking away, and I'm thinking maybe I should announce that I'm the plumber and come out of the stall.... Whoa, I'm wearing a snazzy suit and tie, a little credibility problem here. Twenty minutes pass by. My thoughts started to alternate between amusement and outright terror: "I'm running late for my gig!" "But this is a great story for my book!" "I could get five years for lewd conduct!"

The decibel level on that last thought almost broke the sound barrier as I noticed, in the small space between the stall door and the post, an innocent young female face trying to peer into the crack! If she reports what I think she sees, I may be in for a radical lifestyle change.

Finally, after 25 minutes of protecting my anonymity, the bathroom empties. I quietly arose from the seat, and headed to the door. I cracked it just a bit and scanned the once-again empty lobby. I burst out the front doors of the school with a great sigh of relief. There was a little girl sitting on the steps who looked up at me and smiled. I knew she was the one who saw me in the stall, and I simply lip-synched the words "thank you" to her. She giggled, and replied, "I liked your squeaky voice." (Thank God she had a sense of humor.)

WHERE ATTENTION GOES, A SMILE SHOWS.
Recently I gave a workshop on the Big Island of Hawaii. I had returned my rental car and shuttled to the terminal in Kona, and I was waiting on line to check my luggage when I realized I had left my pocket computer in the car. I walked over to the counter of the car rental company and they phoned the drop-off building. Unfortunately, nobody had found my pocket computer, which stores all my appointments and many telephone numbers.

I was upset, not just over the loss, but because I knew it was ripped off by an employee. I went back to the airline counter to check my luggage, and to add to my chagrin, was told it was too late to put my bags on the flight, that they would have to go out on the next flight. I was not a happy camper!

I boarded the flight looking like a volcano about to erupt. Knowing how such rage and upset can impact my psychological and physiological health, I endeavored to shift my attitude. Across the aisle from me sat two young girls. The one sitting closest to me was drawing something on a paper bag. I decided to focus my attention on her and observed her look of innocence and joy in the creative process. I asked the little girl what she was drawing and she just shrugged. As I watched her, a stewardess announced, "If there is anything we can do to make your flight more pleasant, please let us know." I promptly turned to the stewardess and quipped, "Can we go back and get my luggage?" She laughed, and I felt myself starting to loosen up.

Then the budding young artist across the aisle got my attention and showed me her finished creation, which she had slipped over her hand. It was a barf bag transformed into a puppet with a really wacky face! I smiled at her and congratulated her for a job well done—not only for the creation, but for helping me let go of my funky mood. Kids can be tremendously refreshing when on the road.

BLUSH 'N FLUSH. There is an exercise in my workshop called the Blush 'n Flush, in which people pair up with a partner and share an experience in their life where they felt foolish or embarrassed. One time a man came up to the front of the room after the exercise and related an embarrassing moment from a business trip to Boston. He decided to see a movie one night and noticed that the film *Someone To Love,* directed by his favorite director, Henry Jaglom, was playing down the street.

He went there, but when he looked at the marquis it was not listed. Feeling disappointed, he turned to a couple standing next to him and implored, "Excuse me, I'm looking for *Someone To Love.*" The couple got the wrong impression and backed away from him as the man replied, "We can't help you with that, buddy." When he explained to them that it was the title of a new movie, they all had a good laugh and it helped him to lighten up after a long business meeting.

REALITY CHECK. Travel brochures can be very seductive, making us drool with the desire for exotic, dreamy foreign destinations. Sometimes the heightened anticipation is betrayed by the realities of actually being there. Some amusing examples:

Fantasy	**Reality**
"in the historic heart of the Old City..."	the slums
"old world charm..."	bathroom in the hallway
"room with ocean view..."	picture of ocean on wall
"relaxed pace..."	leisurely room service
"secluded, pristine beaches..."	swarming vendors
"friendly, exuberant natives..."	everyone expects a tip
"architectural masterpieces of past eras"	dilapidated
"haute cuisine..."	undercooked, over-priced snack

If you experience this distinction between fantasy and reality on your vacation, make up your own satirical travel brochure just for the fun of it.

FLOWER POWER. I know a man whose terrific Mexican vacation was almost spoiled by an indifferent customs officer. While in Mexico City, he met a beautiful Mexican woman. She toured him around the city the night before his flight was to leave. The next day at the airport, she surprised him by showing up at the airport to give him a bouquet of flowers as a send-off.

After she left, he went through customs and was stopped because he didn't have a tourist card. They ushered him into the office where a customs official refused to let him go. My friend was desperate to make his flight, but no matter what he said or how much he pleaded, the shiftless customs man wouldn't budge. Frustrated, my friend threw the flowers on his desk. His eyes opened wide as he said, "Para mi?" (for me?). Noticing the change in the man's demeanor, my friend replied, "Si, claro." (sure). The customs official smiled and said, "You can go now!" This is the stuff made for TV talk shows: "Mexican customs official romanced by frustrated flier...next on Oprah..."

Putting the flowers on the desk created a pattern breaker that altered the officer's normal way of being. It allowed for a new opportunity to occur. Who would have guessed that a bouquet of flowers would become an essential tool for leaving the country? Life is full of strange and humorous twists!

PAGING THE REAL OR IMAGINED. The little trickster in all of us can be summoned to add spice and ease boredom in our travels. If you are yawning your way through a long layover at an airport, you can have fun while you wait. During flight delays and between connecting flights, go up to the airline counter and have them page a famous character. Buster Keaton, Ralph Kramden, Edith Bunker, Scarlet O'Hara, and Elmer Fudd are just a few names that have been trumpeted over airport terminal speakers, provoking chuckles from passengers and airline personnel.

It can be very amusing to sit next to someone who has never flown before. When I started writing this book, I decided to poll flight attendants on the most off-the-wall questions they've been asked by passengers:

THE TEN LOONIEST QUESTIONS ASKED BY AIRLINE PASSENGERS

10. Is the food cooked on the plane?

9. If I don't eat, will I get a partial refund on my plane fare?

8. If I don't finish the meal, can I put it in a barf bag and take it home?

7. Could we go back and get my coat? I left it at the departure gate.

6. Does the pilot turn on windshield wipers if it's raining outside?

5. Will the oxygen mask be the right size for my head?

4. Does taxiing on the runway count for frequent flyer miles?

3. Will it get cold when we fly over the North Pole?

2. If I flush the toilet, will it hit someone on the ground?

1. Can I keep my dog in the overhead compartment?

CHECKING IT OUT. When I am hired to speak at large conferences out of town, there is often a long line waiting to check in at the hotel. Such was the case at a recent medical conference in Las Vegas. I was tired upon arrival and the last thing I wanted was a long wait to check in. Twenty minutes later I was at the counter. When the desk clerk asked me if I wanted extra room keys, I turned to all the nurses waiting behind me and shouted, "Anybody want an extra key to my room?" They all giggled, but no takers. I turned back to the clerk and said meekly, "No, that won't be necessary."

WADDLES WITH DUCKS. One time I stayed at the Peabody Hotel in Memphis, reputed to be the most elegant hotel in the city. Indeed, it had a classic Victorian charm. After giving an all-day seminar at St. Jude Children's Hospital, I returned to the hotel shortly before 5 P.M. to find a huge throng abuzz in the hotel lobby, and many more hanging over the mezzanine railing with cameras in hand. I heard there was a movie being shot in town, and figured there must be some celebrities staying at the hotel. More inclined towards snoozing than schmoozing, I made tracks for the elevators. As I maneuvered over there, I noticed a red carpet rolled out between the elevators and a fountain that was in the middle of the lobby.

It was quite the fanfare but I was determined to sidestep it and find refuge in my room. One elevator door was open and when I tried to board it I was stopped by a security guard who said, "You can't get on the elevators, sir." I looked at him defiantly and snapped, "Why not? I'm a guest here." He said, "Because the ducks are about to leave the fountain." I looked at him incredulously, and said, "The ducks?" He replied, "It's a daily practice, sir."

The din of the crowd reached a crescendo as five ducks came waddling out of the fountain and down the red carpet, guided by their trainer. Cameras were flashing everywhere, and the crowd converged to get closer. The guide ushered the ducks onto the elevator, then turned and said, "There's room for two more." I said, "Ducks, or people?" My quip drew laughter from the crowd, and someone suggested that I have the honor of riding with the ducks. How many people can say they took an elevator ride with five ducks at the most elegant hotel in the city?

SLEEPLESS IN ALASKA. This story comes from my friend and fellow speaker, Tom Daly: "I was staying at the Sheraton in Anchorage, Alaska. In the middle of the night, about 3 A.M., this Klaxon horn goes off, like in the military, extremely loud, very annoying. Then this loudspeaker comes on in your room and the fire marshall announces, 'Warning, warning. There's a fire in the hotel. Leave your room immediately!' This message keeps repeating itself. I'm on the fourteenth floor, so the first thing I do is look out the window wondering where's the smoke. Then I run out into the hall in my skivvies where I knocked over three women dressed in bathrobes. They were all in a panic and I tried to calm them down, realizing there was no smoke anywhere. When we all got more mellow and certain that it was a false alarm, we ended up chatting until 5 A.M. and became friends."

COMIC DISCOUNT. Recently I was booked to give a speaking engagement and workshop in Carmel, CA. My girlfriend accompanied me to the gig— we drove up the scenic California coast from L.A., and after my presentation we spontaneously chose to spend an extra day in the Big Sur area. Since it was high season we knew it might be difficult to find a place to stay, and we investigated a few places without success. Then my partner suggested that we try a ritzy hotel her friend had recommended to her. I agreed to at least check it out, so we drove straight there and entered the lobby, which had a woodsy yet elegant ambiance.

We discussed what the absolute price ceiling would be for us, assuming there was a room available, and decided on $200. I rang the bell for the desk clerk, and out came a young woman that I bantered with for starters. She informed us that there was one vacancy—a room with a king size bed, fireplace, large bay window with an ocean view, and a Paver tile floor, for $325. I said, "Do you have any corporate discounts?" She said, "No, we don't." I persisted. "My partner and I both own businesses. Is there a discount for business owners?" She replied, "Sorry." Finally I said, "Any discounts for Jewish comedians?" She pulled her chair back, stood straight up, and with a strange look in her eye replied, "I'll be back in a minute." She swiveled around and exited through the door behind her.

My girlfriend looked at me with her mouth agape and said, "What's going on with her? You think she's going to call security or something?" I said very quietly, "No, I think we're going to get a discount on the room." She reentered the room and announced, "You can have the room for $200." Talk about made to order perfection!

ADVICE FOR THE WEARY. Being on extended trips can get wearisome for frequent travelers. Still recovering from jet lag and the palate-numbing cuisine served on the plane, you arise in your hotel room, wondering which city you're in now, and stagger out of bed in a nebulous haze.

You stumble into the bathroom, turn on the shower, and soap yourself down with body lotion, shampoo your hair with toilet bowl cleaner, and spray your underarms with Lysol. You attempt to reach room service on the blow dryer. For breakfast, you put sugar on the hash browns and pour ketchup in your coffee. Life is a blur of airports, hotels and coffee shops.

If you find yourself getting lonely, bored or fatigued from extensive traveling, carry a tape of your favorite comedian, keep funny photos in your wallet, or find some children to play with. Talk with them, amuse yourself with them. I find it tremendously revitalizing whenever I'm on the road, whether it's work or vacation. A child's perspective is the perfect break for long distance flights, intense business negotiations, or an energizing lift prior to giving that all-important presentation.

Comedian David Brenner has some hilarious travel insights in his book, *If God Wanted Us To Travel*. The following is a partial list of his helpful facts and tips that are not true:

- If you get sucked out of a plane, the distance you travel on your own will be added to your frequent flyer miles.
- If you're wearing Bermuda shorts when flying over the Bermuda Triangle, your ass will disappear.
- English-speaking people who know New York City streets by heart are not allowed to drive cabs.
- If Japanese tourists were to take over the U.S., Disneyland would become the nation's capital.
- Air Iraq gives special rates for Bar Mitzvahs.
- Gas station sinks are actually white.

UNPOPULAR CULTURE. We've all heard that it's not the destination, it's the journey that makes travel (and life) interesting. But it's tough to justify that statement after driving for several hundred miles with little to see. For amusement, get on a side road that takes you to exotic hamlets with names like Bum Screw and Big Wart. Explore the local culture by talking to an old codger named Luke who has leathery skin and sits in a rocking chair on a sagging porch in front of a five-and-dime store. Go to a special event (if there is one, like "The Mold & Mildew Festival" or "Hay Fever Days"). There's a diamond in that haystack somewhere, or at least a funny photo op.

CUSTOMIZED APOLOGY. Some people may get confused about social norms and even proper disposal of waste in cultures foreign to their own. A few years ago I was strolling down Hollywood Boulevard with a lady friend from Down Under. She took a wad of gum out of her mouth and proceeded to throw it in a mailbox. I was confounded by her behavior. "Why did you do that?" I asked. She replied, "Been chewin' it for awhile. Just had to throw it in the trash." I cackled with laughter and said, "But that wasn't a trash container. It was a mailbox."

She felt bad and wanted to wait for the collection person to arrive so she could forewarn him or her about the misdeed. Since that would have taken hours, she stuck a note on the mailbox that said, "Sorry. I threw a wad of gum inside the box. I thought it was a trash bin."

Deepest Regrets,

Tina
Sydney, Australia

THE NATIVES ARE ACTUALLY FRIENDLY. Having a positive perspective towards all people can eliminate built-up stereotypes. The first time I was in France, all the hype about the arrogance of the French people was laid to waste. I was determined to maintain an open, positive demeanor, knowing that it tends to attract the same to me, though admittedly I was stunned by what awaited me in Paris.

Upon my arrival, I was looking at a map of the city while walking through the train station, when a man came up to me and asked me in French if I needed directions, and where I was from. I answered in my rudimentary French, and he gave me directions in his elementary English. Unsolicited help in Paris!? About two minutes later I was again approached by someone offering assistance in finding my way. Ironically, it seemed like every single day I was in Paris, people would come up to me in the Metro and ask **me** for directions. Oh, those doting, friendly French folks!

REGGAE ON THE ROAD. Driving in foreign countries can be a real adventure. The first time I went to Jamaica, I got my first lesson in driving on the other side of the road in a rainstorm. Judging distances on either side of the car was a challenge, which was also complicated by having to dodge huge potholes, and goats crossing the road.

It seemed like a tightrope between hitting an oncoming goat or vehicle, or going into a ditch. I lightened up by making frequent stops for "jerk" chicken and Red Stripe beer, and talking to the locals about my driving difficulties, which prompted the friendly, famous Jamaican response, "No problem, mon!" Of course, none of them owned cars.

MOTOR MOUTH. Author P. J. O'Rourke has certainly been around the world enough to amass some classic tales about driving through foreign countries. In the book *Holidays In Hell* he quotes a character named Ahmed, a Lebanese man who loved to tell stories about Syrian checkpoint soldiers: "A Syrian soldier stops a Volkswagon Beetle and demands that the driver open the trunk. The driver begins to open the luggage compartment at the front of the car. 'No!' says the soldier, 'I said the trunk.' 'This is the trunk,' says the driver. 'I am not a donkey,' says the soldier, pointing to the back of the car. 'Open the trunk!' So the driver does as he is told, exposing the VW's engine. 'Aha!' says the soldier. 'You have stolen a motor. Furthermore, you have just done it because it is still running.' "

LOST IN A FOG. Getting lost in a foreign land can be a bit frustrating. When asking for directions, sometimes I will play with my frustration by initially referring to a place that doesn't exist in that country. In London, England, I asked a man for directions to the Holland Tunnel (which links New York and New Jersey). In an accent as thick as London fog, he replied, "I don't recall a tunnel that goes to Holland...sorry, can't help you out there...I'd be curious to know if there actually is one."

TONGUE THAI-ED. In George Burns' book, *Dr. Burns' Prescription For Happiness*, he relates a funny story about language misinterpretations while traveling with a female companion: "Cathy had been studying her Thai language book so she'd be ready when we got to Bangkok. The first store we went into there had everything. She saw some silver candlesticks she liked, so she took out her little book and tried to talk to the clerk about them. After a few minutes he gave up and walked away. I said, 'Cathy, they all speak English.' She said, 'George, I'm having fun, let me enjoy myself. When in Rome, do as the Romans do.' I replied, 'They speak English too.'

"She wanted to do it her way, and she went through the entire thing again with another clerk. He kept nodding, and she said, 'You understand, don't you?' He said, 'Oh yes. Except for one thing. What are you going to do with a live monkey?' That's when Cathy gave me the book."

LOST IN THE TRANSLATION. As English has become the international language, most countries attempt to translate basic instructions, directions, rules and regulations for the benefit of the English-speaking visitor. Luckily for the traveling humor detective, this earnest, well-intentioned endeavor results in some of the most outlandish signs imaginable, as documented in the book *Anguished English*, by Richard Lederer:

- Detour sign in Japan: Stop: Drive Sideways.
- In a Japanese hotel: Please to bathe inside the tub.
- In a Swiss mountain inn: Special today—no ice cream.
- In a Paris hotel elevator: Please leave your values at the front desk.
- In a Bangkok dry cleaners: Drop your trousers here for best results.
- In a Japanese hotel: You are invited to take advantage of the chambermaid.
- In an Acapulco hotel: The manager has personally passed all the water here.

TRAVEL TRICKS

- Find kids to amuse yourself with.
- Create your own travel brochure.
- Keep funny photos in your wallet.
- Carry tapes of your favorite comedians.
- Look for funny signs, especially in foreign countries.

EPILOGUE
(Written Because My Editor Said So)

By now you might be thinking that I belong in a strait-jacket, and declare that Terry Braverman, with all his wacky ideas, is unfit for human consumption! If someone came up with a viable alternative to viewing the absurdities, incongruities and incredulities of everyday living, I'd be interested. But without a humorous perspective, I'd be snorkeling in this sea of existence with foggy goggles.

If I made it look too easy to access fun and humor in all aspects of our lives, I apologize. It takes a fair bit of inner work. I don't expect you to use all the ideas put forth in the book, because you may eventually get arrested. However, if you use at least one idea consistently, like wearing a clown nose in traffic, singing to your loved ones in an operatic voice instead of arguing, or starting a game show to learn new skills at work, I promise it will make a difference.

Releasing our human tendency to be attached to people, places, possessions, money and outcomes is the ultimate step to mastery of life. There are even people who are attached to being non-attached. We're all one big wacky family.

What I know is this—when I am able to step back from my reactive states and simply observe from an objectively mirthful point of view, my behavioral pattern can appear quite ludicrous to that impartial "observer" within me. Then the possibility opens up to lighten up, either finding humor in the circumstances, or just laughing at my serious posture in relation to it.

I trust that the book will activate the impartial observer in you during trying circumstances and help you to be happy, in spite of it all.

And now, for those of you who already have a full plate—next up, a heavy dose of reality....

PRIME
RIB
TICKLERS
(With Sauce on the Side)

BIBLICAL BLOOPERS

This historical/hysterical perspective comes from the book *Anguished English*. These gems were excavated by teachers throughout America from eighth grade through college level students, and strung together by the author:

"The bible is full of interesting caricatures. In the first book of the Bible, Guinesses, Adam and Eve were created from an apple tree. One of their children, Cain, asked, 'Am I my brother's son?' "

"God asked Abraham to sacrifice Isaac on Mount Montezuma. Jacob, son of Isaac, stole his brother's birthmark. Jacob was a patriarch who brought up his 12 sons to be patriarchs, but they did not take to it. One of Jacob's sons, Joseph, gave refuse to the Israelites."

"Pharoah forced the Hebrew slaves to make bread without straw. Moses led them to the Red Sea, where they made unleavened bread, which is bread made without any ingredients. Afterwards, Moses went up on Mount Cyanide to get the ten commandments. He died before he ever reached Canada."

"David was a Hebrew king skilled at playing the liar. He fought with the Finkelsteins, a race of people who live in Biblical times. Solomon, one of David's sons, had 300 wives and 700 porcupines."

QUIRKY QUOTES

"I have an aura of transparency."—Author

"Guilt is a wonderful thing to waste."—Author

"Lose hair now, ask me how."—Michael Horn

"People are dying to be reincarnated."—Author

"I'm rushing off to my meditation class."—Friend

"I X-ray everything from the head on up."—Nurse

"Sometimes I have a false sense of insecurity."—Author

"To avoid suspicion, never lace your shoes in a melon field."—Chinese proverb

"When my ship comes in, I'll probably be at the airport."
—Author's brother

"I always keep boiled water in the refrigerator."
—Author's mom

Author:	How many times in your life do you meet someone that you really adore?
Ex-girlfriend:	I don't know. I'm not dead yet.
Author:	Are you a vegetarian?
Friend:	Yes, but I do eat pork from time to time.

SIGNS ACTUALLY SEEN

Sign in store window: Sidewalk sale inside.

Sign on fence: Trespassers shall be violated.

Sign on porta-potty: Maximum occupancy—ten.

Sign at church: Jesus Saves.

Sign at adjacent supermarket: Safeway Saves More.

Sign at restaurant/service station: Eat here and get gas.

Sign at shoe repair store: Mistakes made while you wait.

Sign at health food store: I went on a thirty day diet and lost a month.

Sign at store cash register: Prices subject to change based on customer attitude.

Sign at a street curb in the movie, L.A. Story: Libra parking only.

Sign at New Age bookstore: All products come with an unconditional three lifetime warranty.

Sign in front of a pub: Free Beer. (It was the name of the band playing there....Very clever)

STRANGE BUT TRUE:
ASSOCIATIONS HEADQUARTERED IN CALIFORNIA

Lath & Plaster Bureau
California Prune Board
Coin Laundry Association
Sand & Gravel Association
Fuyu Growers of California
Cantaloupe Advisory Board
Scottish Fiddlers Of California
Squab Producers Of California
Dried Fruits & Nuts Association
Tire Retread Information Bureau
International Drapery Association
International Pumpkin Association
Western Society of Weed Science
California Refuse Removal Council
Exotic Dancers League of America
International Dry-Cleaning Congress
International Coil Winding Association
California Cling Peach Advisory Board
California Dump Truck Owners Association
Western Brahma Bulls Breeders Association
California Dairy Herd Improvement Association
American Dehydrated Onion & Garlic Association
National Association of Seventh-Day Adventist Dentists
California Fresh Carrot Advisory Board (advice: stay in the ground!)

IDEAS FOR NEW ICE CREAM FLAVORS
SUBMITTED TO BEN & JERRY'S
(Terry Braverman & Michael Horn)

Liver Mint
Banana Bacon Swirl
Blueberry Turnip Sorbet
Seaweed Almond Fudge
Pineapple Borscht Ripple
Turkey Granola Bar Crunch
Chocolate Tuna Prune Whip

TWENTY WAYS TO LIGHTEN UP

1. Create a joy list (people, places, activities, and things that bring you joy, laughter, pleasure, satisfaction and fulfillment).

2. Be with fun people.

3. Play with children and pets.

4. Start a cartoon board at work.

5. Dress in colorful, outrageous clothes.

6. Use the element of surprise in your life.

7. Take a comedy, improv or acting class.

8. Create a "massage train" while on break at work.

9. Start an acknowledgement board at work.

10. Keep funny photos in your wallet or purse.

11. Get toys and props for the home and office.

12. Start a humor library of books, tapes, videos, etc.

13. Give someone who is having a tough day a standing ovation.

14. Exaggerate your mannerisms and other people's mannerisms.

15. Keep a diary of humorous experiences that occur in your life.

16. Place a mark on your body to show where you've had it up to.

17. Sing your stressful situations in an operatic or country western style voice.

18. Practice Humor Impact Aerobics (silly faces, exercises, wear clown noses, etc.).

19. Be open to unusual, out of place, or funny signs and happenings in your environment.

20. How would_____react if they were in your situation? (the Three Stooges, your mother, Harpo Marx, Lucille Ball, Richard Nixon, a gorilla, etc.).

GIVING CREDIT WHERE CREDIT IS DUE
(AND PAYABLE, IN SOME CASES)

Excerpts in Chapter I.

Page 3. Doran, John. *History of Court Fools.* © 1858 Francis A. Nichols & Co.

Page 4. Hornby, John. *Clowns Through the Ages.* © 1962 John Hornby.

Page 4-6. Sams, Jamie. *Sacred Path Cards: The Discovery of Self Through Native Teachings.* © 1990 Jamie Sams & Linda Childers. Reprinted by permission of Harper Collins Publishers, Inc.

Page 11. Rothchild, Sylvia. *Voices from the Holocaust.* © 1982 Penguin Books. Reprinted by permission of the William E. Weiner Oral History Library.

Page 12. Laska, Vera. *Women in the Resistance and in the Holocaust.* © 1982 Greenwood Press. Reprinted by permission of Greenwood Publishing Group, Westport, CT.

Page 12. Crane, Allison. *Pastor ODs on Laughter* story. Reprinted by permission of Allison Crane.

Page 13. Brown, Robert McAfee. *The Essential Reinhold Neibuhr.* © 1986 Yale University Press. Reprinted by permission of Yale University Press.

Page 13. Winston, Kimberly. *Comedians are Taking Their Act to Church.* © 1995 Tri-Valley Herald. Reprinted by permission.

Page 14. Burkey, Brent. *Laughter Helps Keep the Faith.* © 1995 Marin Independent Journal. Reprinted by permission.

Page 14. Schulz, Charles. *"Nobody would have been invited to dinner as much as Jesus was unless he was interesting and had a sense of humor."* Reprinted by permission of United Media.

Excerpts in Chapter II.

Page 20-22. Cousins, Norman. *Anatomy of an Illness.* © 1979 W.W. Norton & Company. Reprinted by permission of W.W. Norton & Company.

Page 23. Pelletier, Dr. Kenneth. *Mind as Healer, Mind as Slayer.* © 1977 Delta Books. Reprinted by permission of Bantam Books.

Page 25. Chopra, Dr. Deepak. *Creating Health.* © 1987 by Deepak Chopra. Reprinted by permission of Houghton Mifflin Company. All rights reserved.

Page 26. Rogalski, Robin Lynn. *Joke Signals* story, © 1996 by Robin Lynn Rogalski. Reprinted by permission of Robin Lynn Rogalski and dedicated to the memory of her father.

Excerpts in Chapter III.

Page 31-32. Houston, Jean. *A Mythic Life.* © 1995 by Jean Houston. Reprinted by permission of Harper Collins Publishers, Inc.

Page 36. Robbins, Anthony. *Unlimited Power.* © 1986 by Robbins Research Institute. Reprinted by permission of Simon & Shuster.

Page 37-38. Chaplin, Charles. *My Autobiography.* © 1964 Plume Books. Reprinted by permission of Random House U.K.

Page 38. Hornby, John. *Clowns Through the Ages.* © 1962 John Hornby

Page 40. Lewis, Abigail. *Interview with Ram Dass.* © 1996 Whole Life Times. Reprinted by permission of Abigail Lewis.

Excerpts in Chapter V.

Page 54. Simon, Neil. *The Prisoner of Second Avenue.* © 1972 Warner Brothers. Reprinted by permission of Neil Simon.

Page 58-59. Godek, Gregory J.P. *The Portable Romantic.* © 1994 Casablanca Press. Reprinted by permission of Sourcebooks.

Excerpts in Chapter VI.

Page 71. Burns, George. *Dr. Burns' Prescription For Happiness.* © 1984 by George Burns. Reprinted by permission of The Putnam Publishing Group.

Page 72. Kaplan, Robert M. & Pascoe, Gregory C. *Humorous Lectures and Humorous Examples: Some Effects Upon Comprehension and Retention.* © 1977 Journal of Educational Psychology, Vol. 69, #1. Reprinted by permission of American Psychology Association.

Page 75-76. O'Neill, Hugh. *Here's Looking at You, Kids.* © 1996 Simon & Shuster. Reprinted by permission of Scott Meredith Literary Agency.

Excerpts in Chapter VII.

Page 87. Dyer, Wayne. *Everyday Wisdom.* © 1993 Hay House, Inc. Reprinted by permission of Hay House, Inc.

Page 88. Krasna, Norman.*The Marx Brothers in a Nutshell*. © 1990. Reprinted by permission of Robert Weide/Whyaduck Productions, Inc.

Page 89. Rosen, Peter H. © 1980 Creativity Cafe. Reprinted by permission of Peter Rosen.

Page 89-90. Chamberlin, Cindy & Knott, Ronald A., editors. *Accent on Humor.* © 1992 Philanthropic Service for Institutions. Reprinted by permission.

Page 93-94. Wilde, Stuart. *The Trick to Money is Having Some!* © 1989 by Stuart Wilde. Reprinted by permission of Hay House, Inc.

Page 94-95. Hornby, John. *Clowns Through The Ages*. © 1962 by John Hornby.

Page 96. Kaplan, Stuart R. *The Encyclopedia of Tarot, Volume I.* © 1978 U.S. Games Systems, Inc. Reprinted by permission of U.S. Games Systems, Inc. Stamford, CT.

Page 97. Burns, George. *How To Live To Be 100—Or More.* © 1983 by George Burns. Reprinted by permission of The Putnam Publishing Group.

Excerpts in Chapter VIII.

Page 99-100.Kroft, Steve. *Herb and His Airline*. Excerpted from 60 Minutes. © 1989 CBS. Reprinted by permission of CBS News Communications.

Page 109. (See Chapter III, page 36.)

Page 109. Tully, Shawn. *Merrill Bulls Ahead.* © 1996 Time Inc. All rights reserved. Reprinted by permission of Fortune Magazine.

Page 111-113. Ross, Bob. *The Laughter Connection Newsletter, Vol. 2, #4.* © 1992. Reprinted by permission of Bob Ross.

Page 115-116. Eberhart, Elvin T. *In the Presence of Humor.* © 1984 by Elvin T. Eberhart. Reprinted by permission of Elvin T. Eberhart.

Page 117. McCormack, Mark. *What They Don't Teach You at Harvard Business School.* © 1984 Bantam Books. Reprinted by permission of Bantam Books.

Page 124-125. Paulson, Terry L. *Making Humor Work.* © 1989 Crisp Publications. Reprinted by permission of Terry L. Paulson.

Page 125-126. Simon, Neil. *The Prisoner of Second Avenue.* © 1972 Warner Brothers. Reprinted by permission of Neil Simon.

Excerpts in Chapter IX.

Page 143. Brenner, David. *If God Wanted Us To Travel.* © 1990 by David Brenner. All rights reserved. Reprinted by permission of David Brenner.

Page 146. O'Roarke, P.J. *Holidays in Hell.* © 1989 Vintage Books. Reprinted by permission of Atlantic Monthly Press.

Page 146-147. Burns, George. *Dr. Burns' Prescription For Happiness.* © 1984 by George Burns. Reprinted by permission of The Putnam Publishing Group.

Page 147-148. Lederer, Richard. *Anguished English.* © 1987 Dell Publishing. Reprinted by permission of Charles Wyrick & Company.

Excerpts in Chapter XI.

Page 154. Lederer, Richard. *Anguished English.* © 1987 Dell Publishing. Reprinted by permission of Charles Wyrick & Company.

Much effort was made by the author to find the sources for excerpts used. If there is anything that is inaccurate or overlooked that catches your attention, please let the publisher know.

SUGGESTION BOX

Have any great ideas or humorous anecdotes for lightening up? Terry might be interested in using your
material for future publications. You can write them
on this page, and send them to:

Mental Floss™ Publications
3865 S. Grand View Blvd.
Box 661037
Los Angeles, CA 90066

e-mail: mirthpro@pacificnet.net

ABOUT TERRY BRAVERMAN

Terry Braverman is a recovering stand-up comedian (still in recovery), professional speaker, seminar leader, consultant and entrepreneur.

His articles have appeared in national publications, including *Training & Development Magazine*, *Think & Grow Rich*, *Professionally Speaking*, and *Yoga Journal*. Four of his articles have been published in *Whole Life Times,* a monthly publication based in Los Angeles.

The author may be best known as a comic/impressionist who has opened for Broadway and television star Ben Vereen, performed on national television and at the famous *Improv Comedy Club*. As a result of winning the 1991 *Open Audition* (out of 300 acts), he appeared on cable television's *Comedy Central*. He was also in the 1986 television miniseries *Space* that featured James Garner.

As a speaker and seminar leader, Mr. Braverman has presented programs at Fortune 500 companies such as Northrop Corp., Fluor Corp., Baxter Healthcare Corp., and Mosby-Year Book, Inc. (division of Times-Mirror). Other venues include St. Jude Children's Hospital in Memphis, UCLA Medical Center, Hippocrates Health Institute, and several churches as Sunday service guest speaker. His presentations help organizations boost morale, build teamwork, bolster productivity, improve communication, inspire creative thinking and defuse conflict.

SOME HAPPY CAMPERS

Aerospace
"...provided practical and useful tips for integrating humor into your work and life..."
David Hetrick
Organizational Development specialist
NORTHROP CORP.

Education
"...a wonderful demonstration of the therapeutic values of humor...helped to make over 300 of us feel connected and part of a large family..."
James P. Chadbourne, Ed.D.
Director of Educational Services
BRAILLE INSTITUTE

Finance
"...strong communication skills and ability to apply humor in client situations is a real asset in successful marketing for new business. Very entertaining...a rare blend of stand-up comedian and business acumen..."
Bill Sorotsky
Vice President, IMPERIAL BANK

Healthcare
"...evaluations of your seminar were excellent. Participants came away with practical ideas for using humor in real situations....Thank you for reminding us to lighten up..."
Robin Mobley, RN, MSN
Director of Nursing Education
ST. JUDE CHILDREN'S HOSPITAL

Law
"...excellent presentation....Members described your presentation as highly useful for helping them communicate effectively with clients..."
Joe Reber, J.D., LL.M.
President, CULVER/MARINA BAR ASSOCIATION

Manufacturing
"...a real funny guy, but also fills his presentations with provocative content. Terry Braverman would be my choice for any kind of meeting..."
Bill Gove, CSP, CPAE
Former executive, 3M COMPANY

Real Estate
"...for motivation, humor, and how to handle clients, he can give practical skills in a funny, uplifting manner..."
Peter Savio
President, SAVIO REALTY

HOW TO SCHEDULE AN ENGAGEMENT
with TERRY BRAVERMAN

CALL: 310/397-6543
FAX: 310/397-3014

Let us know the date and location of your event and who the audience is, and Terry will create a tailor-made presentation for your group!

MAY WE TAKE YOUR ORDER PLEASE?

Order toll free: 800/304-2847
Fax: 310/397-3014
Order by mail: Mental Floss™ Publications
               3865 S. Grand View Blvd.
               Box 661037
               Los Angeles, CA 90066
e-mail: mirthpro@pacificnet.net

Please send me the following:

	Price	Qty.	Total
Books When The Going Gets Tough, The Tough Lighten Up!	$12.95		
Audio Cassettes Life Is Too Serious To Be Taken Seriously!	9.95		
Warning: Humor May Be Hazardous To Your Ailments	11.95		

Subtotal _____
CA residents: Add 8.25% sales tax _____
Shipping/handling: Add 24% of subtotal _____
TOTAL _____

Company name_____
Your name_____
Address _____
City/State/Zip _____

_ Check/money order
_ Mastercard
_ Visa
_ AMEX

Card #_____
Exp. date _____
Cardholder's name _____
Signature _____

Please make your check or money order payable to:
MENTAL FLOSS™ PUBLICATIONS

LISTEN TO IT WHEN

- Your taxes are due
- Your pants catch fire
- You're stuck in traffic
- Your beagle leaves you

The
Humor Preparedness Kit
for
Health Professionals
and
Those with
Health Challenges

- Boost Morale
- Build Teamwork
- Break Up Conflict
- Break Out of Burnout
- Bring Joy to Your Work